Volume Three
Mystery Mountain
Still More In The Adventures
Of A Mountain Family and
Community As They Do What
Must Be Done
Marie Grace

Author of
The Mystery Mountain Collection
Volumes One, Two, Three and Four,
Thoughts Aplenty

PUBLISHED by PARABLES
Earthly Stories with a Heavenly Meaning

Mystery Mountain, Volume Three
Still More In The Adventures Of A Mountain Family and Community As They Do What Must Be Done
Marie Grace
Author of The Mystery Mountain Collection: Volumes One, Two, Three and Four; and, Thoughts Aplenty

Copyright © Marie Grace

Published By Parables
March, 2018

All Rights Reserved. No part of this book may be reproduced or utilized in any form or by any means, electronic or mechanical, including photocopying, recording, or by any information storage and retrieval system, without permission in writing from the author.

Unless otherwise specified Scripture quotations are taken from the authorized version of the King James Bible.

>ISBN 978-1-945698-51-4
>Printed in the United States of America

Readers should be aware that Internet Web sites offered as citations and/or sources for further information may have been changed or disappeared between the time this was written and when it is read.

Volume Three
Mystery Mountain
Still More In The Adventures Of A Mountain Family and Community As They Do What Must Be Done
Marie Grace

Author of
The Mystery Mountain Collection
Volumes One, Two, Three and Four,
Thoughts Aplenty

PUBLISHED by PARABLES
Earthly Stories with a Heavenly Meaning

MYSTERY MOUNTAIN Three

Dedication

I want to dedicate this third book of my series *Mystery Mountain* to my beautiful daughter, Elaina. She is an excellent mother, caring for my grandchildren with love and nurturing.

Thanks honey for being so wonderful.

Table of Contents

Dedication	1
Table of Contents	2
Karate - The Apartment and an Agreement	5
A Birthday Party Set-up	14
Basketball Team Set-up Plans	21
Roof Fixing & A Red Face	30
A Surprise Party & A Girl in The Woods	35
Informing the Boys & Ira's Heartache	45
Father – Son Advice & A Sad Good Bye	49
A Surprise Gift & A Romantic Dinner	56
More Wedding Plans & A Black Truck	65
Jake Visits Roscoe & Ira Visits Lenore	74
Kid's Basketball Meeting	80
Seven Souls for Christ	83
A Shopping Trip & A Cast Removed	88

First Basketball Practice & Cell Phones	98
First Basketball Game - Ball Park Plans & An Old Printer	106
Seven Baptisms	112
A City Trip & Ball Field Plans	117
Todd Visits Nelli & A Wedding Rehearsal	123
Jake and Angela's Wedding	129
Be My Love Kelli	139
Being A Ronson	145
Todd and Kelli's Wedding Dinner	148
Annabelle's Tragedy	151
Getting His House in Order	163
The Waiting	172
Wedding Plans Continue	176
Legal Work	190
A Wedding, A Bonding Ceremony & Godparents	206

All Scripture references are from the King James Bible unless otherwise stated.

MYSTERY MOUNTAIN THREE

Karate - The Apartment and an Agreement

Jani and Jess seemed to be catching on to the Adrenaline Stress Response Training Jake was putting them through. Jake wouldn't tell Jess, but Jani was picking up the moves faster than he was. However, in Jess's defense, Jake isn't as rough on his little sister's moves as he is with Jess and Ira. Jani has always been more aggressive than Jess, and she really enjoyed jostling with her big brother.

Jani, Jess and Ira have all watched the DVD several times; and are currently digesting the instruction manuals and discussing them as a group. All three seem to be enjoying the engaging and sparring.

Mam often stands outside the room and watches them. Josie is happy they are learning self-defense; but she is worried about her little girl getting hurt, even though Jake has warned Jess pretty sternly not to hurt Jani. Sometimes the thumps and thuds can be heard clear down in the second-floor kitchen.

With Jake's arm still in a cast Mam was surprised that he could do Karate with his imaginary opponent, let alone Ira or Jess. The two big men will practice a while; then head to Jakes project to work.

Todd Carson had been joining the two men on the apartment. His little Toyota Corolla was able to make the path up to the rock; as long as he tightly hugged the mountain. There are so many scrapes on the side of his little car that a few more wouldn't even be noticed. But it's paid for…and it gets good gas mileage – both important on his meager salary. Besides, it seemed to be able to handle the ruts in the forest like a champ.

Jake gave Todd a remote and the pass code - with secrecy orders. Ira Carson had ridden over with his brother to show him the process of entry through the giant rock. It was comical to watch Ira's six-foot-two-inch frame uncurl from the tight quarters of the little vehicle. He was only three inches taller than Todd; but the extra three inches was all legs.

Todd was amazed as Jake showed him through the Judd mountain dwelling. He too had suspected dirt floors and bumpy walls; but the home was beautiful and modern – except for the open pit cook stove in the kitchen. It's been a slow process getting Josie into modern thinking.

"Man, it sure took a lot of work to build this place; it looks like a castle." Todd remarked to Jake.

"Yep, Dad and Mom worked on it for years," Jake responded, "the Bible says a man is supposed to provide for his family and my dad sure has. He even used three-quarter plywood attached to two-by-sixes to firm up the walls; and to attach the elbram. Dad didn't want any walls or ceilings to drop rock or mud on his family. I'm doing the same thing in the apartment."

With the three men working together, the apartment project was nearing completion. The Pella picture windows and door were installed leading to the patio. The 'forgotten' closet had been built; and Jake had installed mirrored bi-pass doors on it so his little red head could see how she looks when dressing. All utilities were now hooked up, and the appliances in place.

Unlike Mam's open pit cooking – Angela will have a stove with an oven. To teach Angela to cook – Mam will have to learn to use one of these newfangled appliances too.

Jake put doors on both tunnel entrances for when he wanted no visitors. He built a scrolled iron fence around the patio. It has spindles an inch apart, and the scrolls are on the outside so little feet couldn't climb on them. The fence is forty-two inches high and painted white to match the rattan patio furniture he and Angela had gotten on their shopping trip to the City.

Jake is so thankful for all the help he has received, especially for Dad's help in welding the fence down in the garage and helping to install it. Plus, with the help of Ira and Todd, the completion certainly sped up; and that means he can marry his love soon…very soon.

It was time for Angela to see their home again. The only time she had seen it was when Jake proposed to her; and it was still pretty rough at that time. He had kept her away during the construction; partly because of all the dirt and dust, and partly because he wanted to be alone with her when she saw the completed project for the first time. Now, wonderfully, there was usually someone working with him, so he was rarely by himself – but - the project was sure coming together faster.

He decided to make a surprise dinner for Angela in their new home. That is, he would ask Mam to please make some lasagna, honey rolls and a salad for them for Friday evening; and leave it in the refrigerator. He would pick up some soda – without caffeine Mam warned him, Angela doesn't need that in her body. Sure looks like Mam is going to be a very protective mother-in-law – and grandmother. It's been years since Angela has had anyone to look after her; she's had to look after everyone else.

That's about to change my little soon-to-be wife, Jake was thinking, *around here you will be the princess that you are.*

Mam and Jani had graciously volunteered to clean everything so their new home would be fresh. Mam was all for having things clean around her grandkid's mother; she doesn't want any problems from bad air or dirt.

As Jake looked at the completed project, his heart was so full of love and gratitude that he fell on his knees and raised his arms thanking the Good Lord.

Deputy Homer was at his desk doing paperwork when Barstow Perez walked in and greeted him, "Good morning Deputy.

I've been thinking and praying about your idea of a basketball court and two teams in friendly competition. Mia and I discussed the whole idea, and we like it. However, there is one change I have to put forth. I'll be involved; but you'll have to lead one team and Wiley the other one. My schedule at the ranch is pretty full right now…And I'm sure Wiley will probably want to coach his two boys anyway."

Homer mulled Barstow's words around before speaking, "Do ya think Wiley has time ta be a coach?"

"He's probably got more time than I do. I can help organize the teams, but you and Wiley will have to coach them. I have trail rides to head up," Barstow replied, "and I'm often gone for an entire day."

"We cain both talk to him if tha's all right with ya, Barstow, I cain call him an' set up a meetin'," Homer suggested, "let me know when ya have the time an' I'll call him – or you can call him – or the Sheriff can call him. - Whatta ya mean by he might have his two boys on the team? Is Wiley gonna ask Annabelle to marry him, or adopt the boys. Does Annabelle know, or the boys, or…"

Homer was on the word slide again, as Barstow cut in, "Good, I'll check my calendar and see when I have some free time and give you a call. Jake will be out at the ranch tomorrow, so I'll ask him to sit in too."

Homer had accidentally gotten into an FBI Wanted List on the computer. The FBI puts felons' pictures out so law enforcement personnel can see and identify them, he reasoned to himself. But, at the moment the deputy saw the actual FBI words come up they scared him to death. He thought he was in a heap of trouble. However, he just couldn't turn the site off; he wanted to see all the criminals' pictures – never know when a deputy might come across a criminal. Homer was just hoping the FBI wouldn't pay him a visit for intruding on their web site.

The phone rang and Homer about jumped out of his skin. Shakily he answered, "Sheriff's Office, Deputy Homer Newman speaking, is this the FBI? I wasn't doin' anythin' wrong - just looking at the crim'nals pictures."

There was a pause on the other end, then Jani's little voice started laughing, "Homer what are you talking about?"

The deputy recognized Jani's voice, but he was shaking so much he could hardly speak. First to be on that FBI site, and now for Miss Jani to call. My goodness, what's gonna happen next, he was mumbling?

"Homer, are you all right?" She asked him.

"Y-Yes, Miss Jani, I hope I'm not in too much trouble for looking at that web site." He stuttered.

Being confused with his strange words, she put him on the speakerphone so Mam and Jake could listen.

"Homer, what are you talking about?" Jani insisted.

"Well Miss Jani, I was workin' on the computer an' tryin' to check for crooks when the computer turned to a red screen with the words FBI site on it. Gosh, it scared me, Miss Jani. I'm waitin' for the Federal Agents to com' 'n' git me. Gosh, I didn' mean to do somethin' wrong, Miss Jani." Homer was off the deep end.

Jake picked up the phone, as Mam told him to behave himself and not torment the young man.

"Homer, this is Jake, what's the handle on the site."

"I don't see no handles of any kind, I guess there's no handles on this site." Homer answered.

The Judd's were cracking up.

"No, Homer," Jake continued, "I mean what does their web site say their numbers are?"

"Oh, ok, Mr. Jake, it says FBI Home," the young man stuttered, "am I in a lot of trouble?"

"Homer, settle down, you are not in any trouble at all." Jake assured him, "You are a sworn deputy and are looking for criminals; it's ok to be checking on any web site, including the FBI one. That's why they have a site showing the criminals, so law enforcement can see who's out there free that should be found and locked up."

"Gosh, Mr. Jake," Homer said with relief, "I'm not in any trouble...Whew, thanks Mr. Jake."

With that Homer hung up.

Jani looked puzzled, she hadn't gotten to ask him what she

was going to. Oh well, she'd be in town tomorrow anyway and would just stop in his office.

She and Angela were going shopping for linens, and Jani was just wondering if Homer or Sheriff Leo needed anything from the City.

As Jani and Angela pulled up to the Sheriff's office in the little pink bug, Homer caught them out of the corner of his eye. He ran to the door to open it for the ladies.

"Good morning Miss Jani and Miss Angela – I guess we won' be able to call you Miss Angela much longer, then we'll have to call you Mrs. Angela, cause you'll be married to Jake – and no longer a Miss but a Mrs. 'cause that's what happens when a girl gets married." Homer sputtered.

Angela chimed in on his word slide, and was right back at him. They completely understood each other.

Jani just shook her head as she watched their conversations with amusement – too many words for her. She knew he would eventually season and not get so flustered when she was around - which was kind of a compliment; albeit funky. She is aware that he just turned twenty-one – still very young.

Somewhere in their dialog, Angela had asked him if he or Leo needed anything from the City; which is the reason they had stopped.

Homer shook his head a bit, "Oh my gooness, Miss Jani, I hung up on you las' night befor' ya could say what ya wanted. I'm so sorry, please forgive me, 'caus I sure wouldn't want to hurt yur feelin's 'cause you're so special to me…ooops" I said too much. He mentally scolded himself.

"Homer, Homer, it's ok, you didn't hurt my feelings." Jani assured him with a coyly executed smile that made his eyes twinkle as he gulped.

After finally getting the fact out that neither the sheriff nor Homer needed anything from the City, the two girls were off in the little pink bug.

"Homer's such a good kid," Angela was saying as they

swayed with the curves descending down the mountain. Jani liked to take the mountain curves a bit faster than she should.

"Yea, kid is the optimum word." Jani replied with a silly grin.

"Wha's optman mean?" Angela asked.

"The best." Jani answered her.

"Gosh, yu're so smart Jani." Angela responded.

Jani smiled, this union with her brother is going to be a fun trip for the entire family.

Angela bought some sheets; a green floral set, along with four bath towels, four hand towels and eight wash cloths. The white dishtowels had cute little ducks on them to match the dishcloths. She picked out a satin comforter/spread that had various shades of blue and green fading in and out, and matching shams.

"I ain't nev'r had thez shams thingies, but they're with th' spread so I guess we use 'em. Hope the spread doesn't keep slippin' off the bed." Angela remarked.

"You'll need four pillows; two to use, and two for the shams, because you don't sleep on the shamed pillows; they are just to look pretty." Jani informed her.

She and Jani tried out almost every pillow in the store, and soon the ladies were laughing hysterically. Angela had never seen a body pillow, but it looked like it took up too much room in the bed and Jake needed that room to move.

"Now you need a mattress pad to protect your new mattress." Jani said as she held up a package saying *King Mattress Pad*, waterproof.

"Jake don' pee the bed, does he?" A wide-eyed Angela asked.

"Oh no, no, it's just in case something spills on the bed." Jani assured her amid giggles.

The girls picked out a complete set of dishes in a box. It had service for four, plates, cups, saucers, bowls and glasses, with the forks, knives and spoons to match. They were Melmac with mint green leaves on them. Jani reminded her that they would be getting gifts at the wedding, so maybe she didn't want to buy too much yet.

What a hoot, this little red headed sister-in-law - Jani was having a ball.

They had lunch before they started back to *Raincroft*. The rain had started again so they put the top up on the car; seems like there has been more lightning and thunder lately than usual. Angela doesn't like lightning or thunder; it makes their mobile home shake.

Orpha has always been really frightened when there was an electrical storm. Before her stroke, Manny always had to hold her during the tumult weather for comfort. But with her dad abandoning them because he couldn't deal with Orpha's condition, the three kids always tried to be sure one of them was home with their mother during a tempest.

Angela wanted to hurry home so her mother wouldn't be alone.

When Jani got home, Mam asked her how her day had gone, and she told her mother, "It was a hoot."

"Being around Angela is always a hoot." Mam remarked as she and Jani took the sheets and linens down to the laundry room to wash them before they put them on the bed. Angela didn't need to smell all those bad fumes that come with new linens.

Mam and Jani removed the plastic wrappings from the comforter/spread, shams and pillows and lay them out on the bed to air. They left the patio door open for fresh air to circulate, but kept the screen door closed to keep out bugs, birds and maybe even critters.

Stria and Oreo soon figured out how to get in the apartment by way of one of the hallways. They loved sitting on the deck and looking over the valley and watching the wildlife as they wandered in to get a drink out of the lake. Mam shooed the rascals back down the hallway to her kitchen while both ladies smiled with satisfaction as they perused the apartment; it was ready for occupancy.

"Our lives are about to change dramatically," Josie told her daughter, "in fact it already has with Angela, Ira and Todd coming in from the outside. And, as soon as Little Joe finishes installing the computers in the family room, we'll be having classes. I'm going to start with English pronunciations. I think I'm even going to invite Homer, since he wasn't able to finish the ninth grade. How do you feel about that, dear? The three guys can come in Todd's little car."

"Homer? That's fine with me; he needs some 'learnin'," Jani snickered.

Now the mystery of entering the mountain would be known to more people; but Mam wasn't afraid of either one of the guys giving out the secret, nor the code.

A Birthday Party Set-Up

Leo picked up the receiver as the telephone started jingling on his desk, "Sheriff Beauregard."

"Leo, this is Wiley," came the booming voice on the other end, "just found out Sonny is having a birthday tomorrow; and turning eighteen. I understand he's never had a birthday party. Is there any way Homer can put one together in the amphitheater for tomorrow? Kid's been working his dang head off - digging footings, water and sewer lines. He doesn't even go home until late. Says he wants to be reliable like Jake."

"I'm sure he will;" Leo responded, "he's right here, talk to him yourself."

The sheriff pointed to the deputy's receiver and Homer pushed the button on line two as he said, "Hello Wiley, this is Homer, what cain I help yu with?"

"I just found out that tomorrow is Sonny Boatright's' eighteenth birthday, and he's never had a birthday party. Suppose you can put one together with such short notice?" Wiley inquired.

"Sure, I'd be glad to do it. I'll call Jake an' he cain let Angela an' the gang know to be at the amphitheater about four tomorrow afternoon if that's OK." Homer responded.

"Four o'clock is fine, but tell everyone no gifts." Wiley affirmed.

"OK, I'll tell everybody." Homer assured Wiley. "Todd an' Kelli cain sing somethin' for 'im - an' Billy cain play his Uke an' sing the Happy Birthday song. I'll call Ira an' tell him what's going on, an' to get Todd an' Billy there early."

Wiley smiled to himself, *Homer sure has organization skills beneath that backward exterior.*

"I can't talk now, Sonny will be right back; he had to go up to the ranch for a pit stop," Wiley cautioned, "but please call The Sweet Tooth as ask Sarah to make a sheet cake that will serve about one hundred people; and to please cut it. My oldest boy, Wayne, is here. It's only a skip to your office from here so I'll send him your way with money for paper products and sodas. We can use my big galvanized tub for the ice and soda. Remember, this is a surprise; tell everyone to not say a word to Sonny."

"Sounds like a great idear." Homer advised him; "I'll get right on it."

Homer paused as Wiley's words registered in his thoughts, Wiley called Wayne his oldest boy…

Wiley gave the money to Wayne and his eyes got as big as dollars, "Wow," Wayne observed, "I get to hold this much money?"

"Pay for the cake too." Wiley instructed him as Wayne literally hopped off at a gallop for the Sheriff's Office.

"Where's Wayne going," Sonny inquired as he walked up.

"He's going to take a walk over to the Sheriff's office and see if anything exciting is happening." Wiley explained to him.

They worked for quite a while before Wiley decided to ask the young man about his education.

"Well, Mr. Wiley," Sonny started slowly, "I dropped out of school in the twelfth grade. I was stupid and rebellious. I sure wish now I would have stayed in school; I would have graduated mid-year with honors because I was moved up a semester. Were you able to graduate Mr. Wiley?"

"Sure did, Sonny, in fact since I wouldn't do any dating I became a professional student and got my Master's Degree in Business Finance. I've thought about going for a Doctorate, but I've got other things on my mind now." Wiley summarized to him.

"Like Annabelle and the boys?" Sonny grinned.

"Yep, like Annabelle and the boys. I've gone bonkers for

Annabelle - like a teenager. When our eyes first met, and I took her and the boys out to eat after the church service – I was hooked. You see, Sonny, I had become resolved to being alone and lonely all my life so I wouldn't put a horrible disease on a wife or offspring. Annabelle has two fine boys, and if she'll share them with me – I'll be complete. I've been asking God for a family – and it looks like he is answering my prayers," Wiley confessed, "I even told the Lord I'd take an ugly wife just to have someone for my own, but he sent me Annabelle; a beautiful lady."

Sonny paused before he went on, "There you go with that God thing like Jake, do you think God really answers your prayers?"

"Absolutely Sonny," Wiley assured the young man, "without a doubt."

Wiley watched the wheels turning in the young man's head for over an hour before Sonny asked Wiley, "So what are you doing with your higher education?"

"I've made a few investments that God has blessed, and they are giving me a good return. So, first and foremost I give God back his tithe; now I will be taking care of my new family." The big man paused before he continued, "I'm hoping one of the boys will pick up a love for real estate ownership, and the other accounting. I've been discussing these very things with God; we're told to be specific in our prayers, so I am."

"What's tithe mean?" The young man asked.

"God gives you one hundred percent of everything you have: and He only asks that you give Him back ten percent of the money He gives you - to further His work on earth. You get to keep ninety percent. That's pretty fair; don't you think?" Wiley inquired of the young man.

"Yea, sure is, except for taxes. So that's what that means – yea, tithe means ten percent doesn't it?" Sonny said thoughtfully.

"That's correct Sonny." Wiley maintained.

"You know, Sonny," the big man added, "if you'd like to get your Diploma or test out for your General Equivalence Test, or GED for short, I'd be glad to help you get it, and I wouldn't gossip about it at all. Apparently, it wouldn't take you very long to get it since you were in the twelfth grade; and then we could see what you would really like to do in life."

Sonny looked at Wiley a few moments, he became emotional. Wiley also knew this kid really hadn't had anyone – before Jake – to care what will happen to him. He had been forced to grow up fast, without ever having the opportunity to be 'just a kid'.

Boys need a man to look up to, and Sonny hasn't had one, Wiley was thinking, *and getting into trouble was the only way he could get any attention. As with so many kids, bad attention is better than no attention.*

The *Bell Well Drilling Company* had almost completed the drilling of Annabelle's new well. Wiley and Sonny had finished running the lines in the trenches. An end was in sight.

"I need to go now," Wiley told Sonny.

"You go ahead; I'll finish doing some clean up before I leave. It's not very far to walk home." Sonny replied.

Wiley chuckled as he nodded at the kid.

Wiley stopped by the Sheriff's Office. Homer and Wayne had just returned from their shopping expedition with all the paper products the whole county would need. But that was all right with the big man. 'His boy' was fitting in.

Wiley had told Wilson he needs to stay home and protect his mom; because that's what a man does, protects the ladies. He didn't think Wilson was too keen on digging ditches because when he mentioned it Wilson had drawn back. Wilson seemed to be more of a 'bookworm', and that's OK. Wayne was more of an outdoorsman and already a great gopher and was obviously enjoying learning the names of various tools and how to use them.

"We paid for th' cake," Wayne told Wiley.

Wiley roughed the kids' hair as he told Wayne and Homer they did a good job.

Wayne had a ball riding on Homer's Harley; and he didn't seem to mind the noise at all. He had never worn a helmet, so Homer had to show him how to strap it under his chin and be sure his ears weren't curled under the side flaps. They had loaded the purchases in the sidecar and would leave them there until morning. No use loading and unloading them, besides if the stuff were in the office in the morning, Sonny would see it. Tomorrow Homer could drive his Harley right up to the serving tables. The soda and ice were paid for and Jerrold Nielsen said he would be happy to deliver them to the amphitheater about three and would plan on staying for part of the festivities.

Now Wiley and Wayne would go get the big tub and take it to the amphitheater so it would be there for the ice and soda.

It was starting to sprinkle again as Wiley's jeep pulled into Annabelle's driveway, so the two men darted inside to get out of the rain. They had picked up subs on the way home. Annabelle had made a jug of ice tea. Wiley squeezed her hand as he handed her the sack of food.

Annabelle had the containers sitting around on the floor again as well as on the counter and beds, to catch water from the leaking roof. Wiley had patched some of the holes, but there was so much more work to be done. The drips were noisy as they piloted into the empty buckets.

Wiley had brought out a television, put it in the boy's room and hooked up an antenna so the boys could watch TV. They had seen TV's at friends' homes and at shelters, but never had a television of their own. As soon as they ate they ran to their bedroom to watch whatever would come in out in these boondocks.

The big man filled in his beautiful lady on the surprise birthday party for the next afternoon, and that he would be over about three to get her. He wanted to be early to help get things set up. He also told her the well on her new property was almost finished.

"The septic tank is set and we've got most of the laterals in place. Now we have to get things inspected," he was telling his spellbound audience of one, "I am so thankful that John Stoddard has a trencher, and Barstow loves to use it. Sure, made our work easier and faster.

"Young Todd Carson did a bang-up job drawing the plans and getting them approved for the Permits. Todd has always had to finagle and fight for everything he has ever obtained, and it's made him pretty savvy and cagey."

Annabelle sat quietly. She kept smiling serenely as she listened to Wiley's every word. As he watched her gazing at him, he wasn't sure if she was just happy, or ready to cry. He knows he's got lots to learn about women. When she squeezed his hand, he knew she was happy.

Thunder and a bolt of lightning snapped through the air and as the mobile home trembled Annabelle bolted. Wiley caught her, and held her for a few moments – for safety…She didn't pull away.

Pitter-Pat, Pitter-Pat.

The buckets were getting more drips now, but not nearly as many as before he did the first repair. Wiley would bring more wet tar cement tomorrow morning; hopefully the rain would let up enough that he could fix a few more roof holes. He was making a mental note where the seepage was intruding.

"Sure will be glad when you get into your new home and are safe." Wiley whispered to the little woman still cradled in his arms – who just stood there soaking up the comfort.

"Wilson would like to go with Wayne to the Sheriff's Office in the morning, so he will be able to keep track of the party set up. Is that ok with you?" He asked the lady snuggled into is chest.

"Thas' fine, I'll be ok, I'm alone all-time th' boys ar' in school." She agreed.

"I'll be around fixing more roof leaks anyway Annabelle," the big man told her, "let's just sit down a spell and talk while we wait for the rain to let up some before I leave."

"Yea, at leas' th' litnin'." She agreed.

They talked about her coming from South Africa when she was a teenager. Annabelle told how she had been married off to Wayne Senior when she just turned fifteen. She hadn't even seen him until the day of her wedding, and he was already sick, so she had to quit school and work. She got pregnant with Wayne Junior almost right away; she wanted him to be born in America, so she worked two jobs to save the money to bring herself and Wayne Senior to America.

"It was so hard, Wiley," she choked up as she spoke, "but both kids ar' American Citizens, an' that makes it worth all th' work. Wayne an' I wen' through th' process an' paperwork, an' we became citizens too. I sure miss my mum, don' guess I'll ever see 'er agin."

Wiley listened intently; he wanted to know all her hurts and good times, so he would know how to best take care of her and the boys.

"Barstow and Mia came from South Africa also; did you know that? Their marriage had been arranged too. Mia says she really lucked out because Barstow has been a wonderful husband, and they fell in love right after their marriage. I understand lots of young ladies never have the blessing of the love of a husband, and are treated very poorly." Wiley expressed with compassion.

When Wiley made the statement of young ladies never knowing the love of a husband - he felt the young lady in his arms quiver.

The big man felt sorry that Annabelle had been saddled with a sick man for her husband right from the start at only fifteen years of age. He knew how devastating it must have been for her.

"Was he ever able to be a dad to the boys?" Wiley asked her.

"No. Oh 'e tried, but 'e wus always so tired an' hurtin' so much that th' boys didn' get much of 'is time," Annabelle told him, "then bouncin' from shelter ta shelter there jus' wasn' much they cou'd do. We nev'r did anythin' fun, no money an' no place to do it. They don' know how to play, an' they didn' even smile til yu started payin' attention to 'em. Wiley – I hadn' smiled for years 'til yu made me smile. Thank yu."

Wiley's heart was breaking, and he was fighting back tears, for the sad life this lovely lady had thrust upon her and the boys, and he held her gently until the rain let up.

Basketball Team Set-up Plans

As Wiley passed the Sheriff's Office on the way back to his shop, he noticed Barstow's red truck and Jake's ATV parked in front of it; so, he decided to stop. Barstow had said Homer wanted to get a meeting put together with the four of them, and this looked like a good opportunity.

"Hello," Wiley said jovially as he walked in, "am I supposed to be here?"

Wiley shook hands with Barstow, Jake and Homer.

"Yes," Homer answered, "we tried to call ya, but yur phone went to messages, so I'm glad ya dropped by. Pull up a chair."

If Jani wasn't around, Homer could keep things pretty much organized; amid his backward ways, he was a smart young man.

"Sheriff Leo is out on a surveillance again, been a couple more house break-ins." Homer informed everyone the reason for the sheriff's absence; "the crooks only take real gold pieces or money; don't damage anything and don't leave any fingerprints, and seem to lock the doors when they leave."

A couple of minutes later Sonny sauntered in and sat down in his cell, Jake could tell he just wanted to be with friends.

"The re'son I've called this meetin'." Homer began.

"Just a moment please, deputy," Jake cut in as he hollered over at the lonely kid in the cell, "aren't you going to join us?"

The young man was grabbing a chair before Jake could even finish his sentence as he announced, "Marcus is here today: and he gets upset with me because I won't drink or smoke with him anymore."

Jake smiled at him, so did Barstow, Homer and Wiley. The kid's countenance changed to happy - he mattered.

"The kids aroun' *Raincroft* aren' havin' enough ta do ta keep 'em out of trouble, so we wanna start a couple of fr'en'ly competition basketball teams. Barstow said he will head it up if he can get yur help with the coachin'. We thought Wiley could take one team to coach an' me the other. Since Sonny writes so good he can be scorekeeper, an' a fill in coach if Wiley or I ar' busy, an' Jake can keep thin's fixed. Ain't said anythin' to Sonny yet, needed some solid info first for 'im." Homer continued.

Remembering Annabelle's statement that her boys didn't even know how to play, Wiley jumped at the idea, but reminded the fellas that both his boys would be playing on his team.

Everyone nodded in agreement.

"You been praying for this too Mr. Wiley?" Sonny asked earnestly.

"Well, after this afternoon I sure am." Wiley responded.

The 'fellas' knew there was a deeper meaning to Wiley's words, but didn't pry.

"That sounds like a good plan, Homer," Jake chimed in and everyone else followed suit.

"I need idears for times an' dates for practice an' games an' we need new regulation hoops an' poles an' scoreboards. We'll need seats for the audience, so maybe we can put the hoops in the Town Square. When I was surfin' the Net I saw rolling hoops that can be moved when they'r' not bein' used. I cain ask Roscoe to get permission for us to play in the *Town Square* so's all the people will fit since they can't all fit in *DoSoPa*. But the hoops there in the Park ain't right and we need to think about new ones anyways. I know we has a surplus in the Town's money that coud work. How soon can we start?" Homer laid out the proposal in his usual 'wordy' manner.

"Tell you what," Barstow said thoughtfully, "I have to go to the City day after tomorrow, so I can look at some sports equipment at that time; Sonny perhaps you can ride with me?"

"That's not so good, Mr. Barstow," Sonny replied, "I've got the County coming to inspect the well and septic at Miss Annabelle's new place. I was going to surprise Mr. Wiley by handing him the approvals. They are supposed to be here Wednesday between noon and five in the evening, couldn't nail it down any closer. How's Thursday?"

"Sounds good to me," Barstow replied, "the supplies I have to pick up can be gotten any day this week. We can leave about eight o'clock after I finish chores, if that's ok with you Sonny."

Sonny readily agreed, and he was surprised that Mr. Barstow had asked him if it was okay with him. Being on the right side of the law is really feeling good.

"I'll talk to Roscoe." Jake remarked. He had been looking for a reason to get into a 'chat' with Roscoe anyway; about Beth's ups and downs. He knew there was something deep seated that was really troubling her. He's watched her space out at the ranch and even wipe tears away. He's also seen her early in the morning with her eyes red and swollen as if she cried all night. And something about her always rubbing her arm is disconcerting to him.

"As far as teams, I suggest we post flyers around town for a Basketball Organizational Meeting on Saturday evening about five – at the amphitheater - if that's all right with you guys." Jake suggested.

All agreed, Saturday night would be the first ball game meeting, and they could choose team players at that time. Jake suggested that Todd Carson could make up a nice flyer, probably overnight. Homer could copy the flyers and each of the five men at the meeting could scatter them around town.

Jake took out his cell and called Ira - who handed his cell to Todd - who didn't have his own yet.

Todd loved the idea of basketball teams, and said he would have the flyer to Homer in the morning.

"That kid doesn't mess around," Barstow remarked, "I'm not sure he even sleeps if he's got a job to do. If he decides on something, he'll move heaven and earth to accomplish it."

As Sonny was leaving he noticed Pam sitting on the amphitheater steps logging in her little spiral again.

He walked over to her and greeted her with, "What in the

world is so exciting that you have to write it all down?"

"Just life," she responded, "real life is full of surprises, critical and good experiences and interesting facts."

She didn't seem in the mood for talking; she takes her journalizing everything seriously. Sonny could remember seeing Pam just walking around town many times, watching people and writing in her book; his curiosity was continually being hipped. Every time he saw her, he was memorizing her every move. Sonny was enthralled at her extensive vocabulary. Since high school the dictionary had become his evening 'reader', and now when she said a word he didn't recognize, he would make a mental note of it and go to the dictionary for its meaning and correct spelling when he got home. He had also started studying building plans on the motel's computer late at night as he waited for late night guests.

When Jake got back to the ATV he called his little red head, "Hi baby, I'll be there in a few minutes, can't stay long, but just want to hold you a bit."

He was already on his way.

As he pulled in Angela's driveway, here she came. "I'm gonna miss these welcome's after we get married." Jake whispered in her ear.

"The new one's 'ill be even better," she cooed to him.

"Friday evening I've got something special planned; I'll pick you up about four my love, if that's alright." Jake inquired of her.

"I'll be waitin'." She said as she kept kissing his neck – and breathing into his ear.

"Gotta go my soon-to-be-wife, we aren't married yet." Jake softly informed her as he peeled her off.

Jake, Wiley, Wayne and Wilson arrived at the Sheriff's Office about the same time next morning - six-thirty. Wayne and Wilson went to the cell and sat down like Wayne is supposed to. Wilson was trying to act like a criminal; looking mean, he had never been in a jail cell before, and it was neat – as long as it was play.

Wiley was grinning as he watched them, yes sir; he loved

to watch 'his' boys, and each time he witnessed a small bit of their imaginations come to life, it really thrilled him.

Homer and Leo were already doing paperwork.

"Work's never done until the paper work's done." Leo said as he greeted them, trying to hide the file he had on his desk.

Sonny came in shortly after the two big men, and went to his cell after nodding at both of them to wait for orders. The other four boys came in early too. They seemed to have started enjoying being 'in jail'; there was always something happening.

Jake looked over at Wiley and winked. Wiley winked back. Leo caught the winks.

Jake hollered over at Wiley, "I'm taking Sonny today."

"No, you're not, I am." Wiley shouted back.

The two men put up their 'dukes' as Homer grabbed the cell keys and ran into the cell with Sonny. He locked the door behind him, and then threw the keys to the other cell telling them to lock the door too.

"You're just a windbag," Jake continued at Wiley, "a buffoon."

"You can't fight your way out a wet paper sack," Wiley was coming back at Jake, "you just try and act big but you're not so hot, I can whip you with one arm tied behind my back, especially with you being a one-armed weakling."

Sheriff Leo just kept on working and ignoring the fight.

As the two big men kept spouting threatening remarks at each other and dancing around the floor like one was going to take a swing, they both could feel the hair on the cell visitors standing up in fear. After about five minutes of fighting the two stopped, high-fived each other and started cracking up.

"You guys have been 'Triffled'." Both said at the same time.

The tickle-bug hit the cellmates when they realized there was really no fight, just some excitement for the morning. Everyone was laughing so hard that they were stumbling around with tears in their eyes.

"That wasn' very nice o' ya guys," Homer was complaining

to them as he unlocked the cell doors, "you scared us!"

"That was the idea." Wiley tittered among cackles.

Sonny came out of the cell and chuckled, "Who's really taking me?"

"You'll go with Jake because I've got some more roof repair to do," Wiley grinned non-chalantly, "I also want Wayne and Wilson to go with you, Jake, to see what you are going to show Sonny."

Wayne and Wilson had come out of the cell and Wayne poked Wiley on his side for 'Triffling' him. Wiley gave both of his boys a big hug.

"You didn' seem worried at all Sheriff," Homer exclaimed to Leo, "the big men could 'ave torn this place apart if they'd a fought."

"I know." Leo answered unconcernedly, evidently having seen the show before.

Sonny didn't ask Jake where they were going, he was just glad to be with his big friend.

Wayne and Wilson both were asking, and Sonny told them, "You'll find out when we get there."

The boys had seen the camouflage ATV many times, and had always wanted to ride in it, and now they were - in the rumble seat. What a blast as Jake headed off-road into the woods over humps, bumps and rocks, and straight for the canyon on the west side of town; just opposite from where the boys were used to going.

They hadn't gone too far into the woods when they came upon a construction site. A large sign in front read, *'Future Home of Canyon Casas.'* There were four concrete foundations, two in front and two behind, with several sets of utility pipes sticking up through the concrete in each one. Trees encompassed the four concrete pads. The builders were evidently trying to save as many of the beautiful green trees as possible.

Jake stopped in front of one of the foundations, as he said to his riders, "We're going to start you guys working on this project. And Sonny, I'm going to see what kind of management skills you have because you are going to head up the project as soon as you finish Annabelle's spread. I'll be gone on my honeymoon, but Wiley and I still want buildings one and two finished ASAP, at least by fall.

"We've ordered most of the sticks for the first two – precut – and a semi should be bringing them sometime later next week. We want double thirty-pound felt on the roof for utility expense control. We're using three-fourths inch ply on the roof and sub-flooring. The roof trusses will be on the semi too. We are doing hip roofs."

"Where's the plans, Jake." Sonny asked.

"The Construction Set is there in that clear plastic tube. Todd drew up the plans and got everything permitted. Wiley has a complete set; and my dad and I each have one. I'll give you the construction site set to study until I can get you your own set, so long as you get them back into their tube quickly." Jake cautioned him.

"Wiley, Dad and I have been praying and thinking about something we would like for you to consider. If you like the work and do a good job, instead of paying for your services, we want to Deed one of the units over to you, just like we did Todd for his work. Pick out the one you want. Todd has the northwest upstairs suite in Building One – which overlooks the Canyon. The same Casa in Building Two also overlooks the Canyon if you're interested. Think about our proposition and let us know."

"Did your God tell you to get me stabilized in life?" Sonny queried as he bounced out of the ATV and pulled the Construction Plans set out of the plastic tube it was encased in. He started calculating everything on the plans as he stepped off the foundations. Wayne was also pointing out items on the plans.

Sonny was deep in thought as he questioned, "You guys are doing the work, but who's the actual builder?"

"Wiley and I are the builders," Jake informed him, "we need some affordable housing around here. Each unit has eight efficiency apartments, four on the bottom and four on the top with its own individual utility meter, so occupants will deal with the service companies themselves. However, the sewer and water will be included with their monthly maintenance fees and rent payments. My dad, John Judd, owns a lot of land around here, and he's a silent partner with us. He gave us the land, and we are to put up the buildings."

Wayne was trying to figure out what Sonny was doing as he finished stepping off the foundations.

After several minutes, Sonny looked at Jake as he remarked, "Looks like each building is about fifty-by-fifty-feet... With a four-foot hallway down the middle it would make each unit approximately five-hundred-seventy-five square feet, minus the allotment for the two by six walls. This will make each one approximately twenty-two by twenty-four feet inside. Not very big, but if designed right could be very serviceable. I've seen these combination half-spiral stairs Todd has on the Plans. They are only forty-eight inches wide, and spiral at the bottom, but have four flat stairs at the top. They only take about seventy-two inches of wall space, even with the four-foot well. If you put the older folk on the bottom and let the younger ones climb up the stairs it should be all right.

"Needs picture windows in the Casa's that actually open to bring in furniture if necessary. Todd was smart to put the J-bolts four feet apart. That makes for a lot stronger stem wall than those that are eight feet apart. With the wind gales we get here in *Raincroft*, a solid foundation is really necessary. Good thinking to use two by six sticks."

His big friend was amazed as he replied to Sonny, "Wiley said you are good with calculations, but he didn't say you are extreme. I'm certainly impressed. Where in the world did you learn to calculate construction projects like that, Sonny?" Jake asked the young man, "Wiley, Todd and I worked together on the plans, but it was Todd's idea to put the J-bolts four feet apart. You like that idea, huh?"

"Yea, sure do," Sonny answered - still investigating, "since I haven't had time to go out anywhere I've been working on the Web, studying Structural Development. I really like working in construction."

Sonny walked around all four foundations several more times, examining everything. Wayne was right on his tail.

"How'd you dig the trenches?" Sonny asked Jake.

"John Stoddard is very gracious about letting us use any of his equipment," Jake responded, "he too recognizes the need for some affordable housing.

Sonny was touched again by how the people of *Raincroft* take care of each other – and they all believe in their God – and pray – is there really something to this Bible stuff? He wondered.

Looks like the real estate bug could already be nipping at Wayne, Jake thought to himself, *which will tickle Wiley.*

"I guess we'll go on over to Lane Lumber and nose around for things we might need," Jake remarked, "I need to check on a couple of projects in the woods also, on the other side of town. We'll head over there after we leave the lumber yard."

I really need to keep Sonny away from town today. Jake was thinking.

Sonny watched as Jake and Harvey greeted each other with a nod. Without a word Harvey seemed to know what Jake needed to look at. It was almost as if they were reading each other's minds. Another thought hit Sonny, were they just 'visiting' each other…

The two men sat down in chairs opposite each other as the two boys – and Sonny – rummaged through things. It was almost like three kids in a candy factory; they were each looking for the treasure they knew was lost in the piles.

Jake stood up, nodded to Harvey and headed to the ATV. Sonny was still trying to comprehend the silent visit. Most unusual.

Roof Fixing & A Red Face

The rain had let up overnight. Wiley headed for Annabelle's to patch more holes in her roof. She had coffee ready for him when he got there. He gave her a 'hello' squeeze and sat down at the table. The place smelled really musty, and the miscellaneous containers were all full of rainwater.

"I was jus' gettin' ready ta empty 'em." Annabelle told him.

"I'll do it as soon as I finish my wonderful coffee." Wiley replied.

"Glad ther' wasn' too much lightnen' an' thunder after ya left." Annabelle confessed.

"I'm sorry I had to leave, and that you are so frightened of storms." Wiley told her as he squeezed her hand. He finished his coffee, then grabbed the cans and buckets of rainwater and emptied them. Annabelle reached out her arms like she was going to help him, but he smiled at her as he said softly, "I've got them Annabelle."

Wiley took the ladder and wet tar out of the Jeep and headed for the roof. As he worked he was so glad that her new home had forty-year shingles on it that would keep her and the boys dry – and safe – for a long time. It would also keep the mold from growing like it is on her floors. He was so thankful to Sonny for setting up the meeting with the County for the permit approvals. He was also thankful that the young man was doing so well.

This precious man was happy to be working for 'his' family, even on this old roof. He had worked about an hour and a half when Annabelle appeared on the ground below him. As he looked down at her she had something red all over her face.

It scared him; he thought she was injured - when she hollered up at him, "I's jus' wonderin' if ya know I 'ave lips."

He was stumped and didn't know how to respond. She headed back inside. Wiley beat her to the door.

As he looked at her he could see lipstick - forming lips from under her nose to her chin and over onto each cheek almost to her ears.

They both stepped inside as he took her waist and asked, "What in the world are you doing?"

"Well, ya big lug, I wasn' sure ya notice' I got lips." She teased at him coyly.

"I, ah, well, ah." His words failed him.

"Don' ya wan' ta kiss me?" She asked him.

"Yes Annabelle," he answered quickly, "but I want to be sure it is because you want to kiss me too and not because you are beholding to me."

"Well Wiley Ronson," she cooed, "if I don' know wha' ya feel like ta kiss, how 'ill I know if I wanna or not?"

Her reasoning didn't make sense to him, but she is very much a woman – and he's acutely aware that he has got a lot to learn.

He was holding her closer and closer. Finally, he confessed to her, "Annabelle, I've never kissed a girl. I don't know how."

Twinkles invaded her eyes, and her red face seemed to smile all over as she looked up at him for a few seconds; she could feel his heart pounding now.

He was serious as he continued; "My mother died at childbirth when I was only four years old, and my new little sister died with her. My dad got *Sickle Cell Disease* and I had to take care of him by myself. He died the horrible death when I had just turned sixteen, and I swore then I would never put a wife or child through that.

"Dad had taken out a large Life Insurance Policy before he was diagnosed with SCD. When I received the money, I invested it since I had no one to spend it on.

"My dad's blacksmith shop was paid for, building and all. God has blessed me mightily; and the money just keeps growing.

I plunged into work and education, and kept to myself, building a rough shell around me so no one would know how deeply I hurt. Jake's the only one who could ever see through me, and even though I've got a few years on him, we've become very good friends. Friendship is ageless."

Annabelle hung on his every word. Thoughts good and bad were running through her head as she pondered what Wiley had said as they held each other close. It felt so good to be in his arms, she was safe and cared for, and he just felt right.

"Wiley, this is how ya kiss a lady." She finally said as she gently pulled his head down to her level, and softly put her lips on his.

Wiley caught on fast as he kissed her back. It was even more wonderful than he had always imagined. Her lips were so soft. He felt giddy, lighthearted, and wonderful. He was almost afraid that his heart would bust right out of his chest.

She pulled back as she said, "I like kissin' ya, it felt good an right, an I feel funny."

"Wow, didn't it." He whispered as he initiated the next one.

He didn't know what all these feelings were, they made him feel jittery and out of control, but he sure liked them. Wiley always had to be in control, but right now he obviously didn't have the upper hand.

She seemed to like the feelings also, because she kept coming back for more as she whispered to him, "I'm not doin' this 'cause I'm oblige' Wiley Ronson, but jus' 'cause I tried ya an' I like ya."

She planted another kiss on his waiting lips.

They held each other for over an hour before he told her he had to get back on the roof before it started raining again. Holding a woman was really something.

"We'll do this ag'in, right?" She smiled at him.

"You bet." He assured her as he took off out the door and back upon the roof, closer to the clouds his head was already in.

"Think I'll go over and talk to Barstow for a bit." The cow-eyed man was sighing to himself as he climbed down the ladder, almost without realizing he had.

As Wiley pulled into the ranch, Barstow came over to meet him and started roaring with laughter.

"What's so funny?" Wiley asked him.

Barstow turned the rearview mirror around so Wiley could see his face. It was all red.

"Looks like you sipped the soup Wiley." Barstow said still cackling, as Wiley was busy cleaning the lipstick off of his face. He smelled her sweet fragrance on the rag, so he put the kerchief in his shirt pocket.

"That'll be there for a while, huh?" Barstow grinned.

"Yea, and I need to talk to you – about the birds and the bees, and how women automatically know how to be coy, Wiley told his big friend, "she kissed me, and I kissed her back, and I felt so funny, things were happening to me and – and – I need some advice."

Barstow hugged his friend's neck as he said, "Let's go over there and sit on the edge of the canyon - since you are jumping into one. How much do you want me to tell you?"

"Everything, I've never had any kind of a talk about male and female stuff." Wiley implored him.

Barstow took in a couple of big breaths as he started with the innate differences between male and female - from toddlerhood.

They discussed everything openly and honestly, even covering female monthly visits and emotions. Wiley was telling him what the Bible says about a man and woman's relationship, especially a husband and wife's. He also told him the marriage bed is undefiled, but only the marriage bed. Wiley got that point.

Barstow especially cautioned his friend, "To never discount a woman's intuition. God put in women the ability to size up a person or situation quickly…and better than a man can. Plus, He gave a woman the ability to keep track of a multitude of 'things' at the same time…probably because they generally have to keep track of several kids at once."

The two men talked for over two hours. Barstow was being 'big brotherish' and patient with all of Wiley's questions, and there were many.

John Stoddard had been working by the big barn, and seemed to instinctively know what was going on and made a special point of staying away. Mia had also peeked out a few times, but stayed in the house.

"So, you see, Wiley, you can't just decide what you are going to do without talking things out with Annabelle. Like when you came and told me you were going to marry her, and I asked you if she knew it - and you said no." Barstow was reminding him, "I know how many prayers you have said, and it looks like God may be giving you this family. However, you've got to win over the boy's first – not last. They are an integral part of Annabelle! They are almost adults now, and a happy marriage to Annabelle will depend a lot on how the boys will accept you, and their feelings count greatly. Plus, she has to be sure she wants you too."

"I know, Barstow, but not out of gratitude. I don't want her gratitude, I want her love. I already adore the boys; I would take them even without Annabelle." Wiley told his friend.

Barstow hugged him again as he cautioned the young man, "I doubt that she was in love with her first husband; sounds like it was just a bad arrangement, but she was true to her commitment. So, I suspect some of these feelings will be new to her too, and you have to take the lead to keep things in check. Always remember, a woman is ruled by her heart."

Wiley nodded yes and added, "Now, I've got to pick up my sweetie for Sonny's surprise birthday party. You're coming, aren't you?"

"Sure am." Barstow responded.

A Surprise Party & A Girl in the Woods

People started arriving at the amphitheater by three o'clock, seemed like no one wanted to be late. The whole world loves a surprise party, and even though everyone was told not to bring gifts, many did. Angela and Kelli were already there setting up, and Todd was waiting to practice a song for Sonny – or two or three – whatever he could maneuver with Kelli. Jake had been instructed to show up at exactly four o'clock. Wayne and Wilson wanted to be early to help set up, but with everything they were seeing and hearing, they had forgotten about the set up.

Wayne was still blown away at Sonny's knowledge and he asked him, "Sonny, where did you learn everything?"

"Watching and listening with my two eyes and two ears." Sonny responded.

Jake wondered if he had heard Mam say that since it is one of her favorite sayings - one he has heard all his life. God gave you two eyes and two ears, that means you are to watch and listen twice as much as you speak! He was trying to remember if he had remarked the saying to Sonny, but he couldn't remember doing so. Perhaps he heard her say it at the Exchange?? Any way it is a good word of wisdom.

Pam had decided to sing a song for Sonny too, so she checked with Mr. Bloom about bringing his piano out into the square. He was really all right with it; parties are about his only fun in life now.

Todd, Ira and Billy would all three be there, so plenty of muscle was available. Pam had decided on *'For He's a Big Man Now'* and Kelli would accompany her on the piano. However, instead of He's a big man now, she would substitute *'For Sonny's a Big Man Now'* and that ought to tickle him. She would have to say it fast because it takes more notes to sing Sonny than he's.

When Wiley pulled into Annabelle's, she came out to the jeep to greet him.

"Hi Wiley," she said coyly, "glad ur back."

She kept looking at him like he was supposed to do something. She got tired of waiting, so she planted one on him. He returned her welcome gratefully.

Yep, I've got a lot to learn. He thought to himself as he checked in the mirror. She looked lovely in a white linen slack suit, with a pink barrette in her hair. Wiley could tell even though it was clean that the suit had gotten a lot of use and the buttons didn't match.

When she becomes my wife – she'll be the best dressed woman in town, he told himself, *and so will my boys.*

There he goes again – taking liberties – but he just can't help it.

Pitter-Pat, Pitter-Pat.

The square was noisy as Jake pulled right up into it with the ATV. Cheers for Sonny were coming from everywhere, and a banner was hanging in the amphitheater saying *'Happy Birthday Sonny.'*

Sonny couldn't believe his eyes. Almost the whole town was there – for his birthday? He got really choked up and emotional, but that's all right, because Jake, Ira and Wiley do, and if they do something – it's okay.

Sonny could see Pam walking up toward him and he lost thought of other things around him as she spoke and gave him a 'hello' hug, "Happy eighteenth birthday, Sonny, now you're a grown-up."

"Whew," was the only thing he could get out, "whew."

Carrie was taking pictures with Jake's digital camera, and

she got a good one of Pam giving Sonny a hug. Pam was the one who had gotten the banner.

The neat marble cake had candles on it amongst the little tools Sarah had put all over the top - along with the *Happy Birthday* logo.

Pam saw the tears in Sonny's eyes, and she gave him a longer compassionate hug. Everyone else was coming to give him a hug too. He was grateful for everyone's congratulatory hugs, but he wished they wouldn't have rushed Pam.

Todd was almost the last one to come up to Sonny, and he actually gave him a bump hug.

Sonny couldn't believe it, and he didn't know what else to say to Todd, so he blurted out, "I understand you are the one who spotted where the J-bolts would go."

"With the wind, heavy snow and sometimes steep weather changes around here, I figured it better to be safe than sorry." Todd responded.

Pretty soon they were walking toward the amphitheater set up talking about the project like two men. Jake was pleased; Todd was finally building trust in Sonny.

What sounded like a meadowlark rang out over the speakers, and Todd lost Sonny completely as Pam started singing a birthday song just to him. He had never heard such an amazing voice, and it was coming from this very beautiful lady. He watched her in awe.

Todd stopped trying to communicate with him; Sonny was just too far away.

Jani had stepped up to the table to light the candles on the cake. Homer was not too far behind her; it's up to him, being the deputy, to be sure no fires start, or anyone gets burned. He was still afraid to get real close to Jani; he knew her big brother was watching. But he was close enough to smell her.

People watching kept wondering what he was doing leaning his head toward her, then pulling it back – was his neck hurting or was he just exercising it. Jake knew Homer was sniffing his sister, and he thought it was funny. Ira seemed to know too as the two men exchanged silly glances.

When the candles were all lit, Pam ushered Sonny to the table to make a wish and blow out the candles.

"Make a wish." Pam was encouraging him.

He paused as he looked at the beautiful cake. He'd never had a Birthday Cake, and his name was right on top. He counted the candles, yep, eighteen. The cake was so beautiful he didn't want to have it ruined by eating it – but that's what it was for. So, he made a wish, took a big breath in, and blew all the candles out at once.

"Now," Pam was informing him, "you can't tell anyone your wish until after it comes true; or it won't."

His eyes were fixed on her hazel eyes as she spoke to him.

"Let's eat." Jake broke in. Having two men under spells could have delayed the festivities, and he wanted to see what presents Sonny received.

Jani had put plastic gloves on, so Homer did too. Homer helped Jani pull the candles off the cake, and he licked the frosting off of each one before he tossed it into the trash can. He was pulling the plates apart, with difficulty since paper plates have a tendency to stick together, and handed them one by one to Jani.

Jani asked Sonny which piece of cake he wanted; since he is the 'Birthday Boy' he gets to pick out any piece he wants, even right out of the middle; and be served first. He pointed to a piece that had a cute little hammer on it, so Jani dug it out for him.

Pam led Sonny over to the gift table. There was a chair on the side of the table, and he looked around to see who was going to sit in it. Everyone started laughing as Pam pointed at him and patted the chair. He sat down and Carrie asked him to hold still until she got a couple of pictures.

When he started opening gifts, Kelli and Todd started singing. She was playing the piano, and Todd was sitting beside her as they sang – a bit close Ira commented to Jake.

Leslie poked Ira and told him to behave. Ira was still carrying Leslie around, even though she could maneuver her crutches quite well by herself. He usually didn't give her a choice; before she would realize it, she would be airborne. She would be heading back home Saturday morning, and Ira wanted to enjoy her as long as he could.

Most of the gifts Sonny received were tools, which he was delighted with. Pam was writing the gift list with the names and items. Carrie got pictures of everything.

Kelli and Todd were only going to sing two songs, but they kept singing. Seems as though they just like singing together.

Homer was carrying the sacks of trash to the big container; he didn't think Jani should be lifting heavy things. His head was still moving forward and back as they worked. Jani noticed Homer was filling out more and more as she kept non-chalantly giving him the once-over.

Homer noticed her watching him so he informed her, "I've made me a gym in my back yard. I got differen' sizes o' trees an' logs I'm liftin' an' I'm runnin' 'bout five miles each day. I'm practicin' sayin' my A, B, C's as I run so I can be sophisticated like you."

Jani was touched with Homer's efforts, especially having learned the word sophisticated, but she did wonder if he even knew what the word meant.

"So, the phrase I've heard about you 'pumping stumps' is your exercise equipment?" Jani asked Homer.

"Yes, Miss Jani, I'm working real hard to get strong enough to take care of you." Homer advised her.

Jani was almost speechless as they finished cleaning up. Each time their eyes met, they could feel each other.

As soon as Homer finished his chores for Jani he darted over to the office and came back with a handful of flyers about the basketball teams try outs: scheduled for Saturday at five in the evening. He passed them out to several people to put up around town and on counters in stores. The flyer Todd had put together over night was a really nice one, showing hoops and kids playing and a ball showing action streaks flying away after it had hit the net.

Homer had printed the flyers on mint green paper.

Sonny watched as Pam grabbed a flyer and stuck it in her pocket.

The birthday boy opened a rather large container from Jake and Angela, and Wiley and family. It was a red tool chest, with wheels on bars that dropped down and locked into place. It could be work height and then its legs would fold up underneath it for transporting. He absolutely loved it.

"You'll need that to work on your new projects." Jake hollered at him.

The young man was overwhelmed with gratitude; in the back of his mind he was wishing his sister Donna could have joined the festivities. He missed her being there. She runs the motel when he is gone, under protest, and never associates with anyone - not even him.

When he gets back to the motel each evening, she immediately goes to her room and locks the door. Donna is very grieved that her folks told her that no matter how bad she feels, she will run the motel while her brother is incarcerated. Sonny has tried to force a talk, but it has never worked. It is a lost cause to try to force-talk a woman; they will only withdraw more. He feels so bad for her infirmities, but there just isn't anything he can do. He's not ashamed of her; and would be glad to take her anywhere with him – if she would just go.

Sonny does the grocery shopping, buying lots of microwave meals and he stocks their refrigerator. They are 'set up' on a dispensing machine route, and a man comes weekly to restock the pop and snacks machines; and pick up the money. His sister has plenty of food available to her. She certainly doesn't have to live on snack foods – microwave ones are bad enough. But she will not listen to him.

He would love to take her out to the *Canyon Steak Corral* for a complete meal, but she refuses.

Mike Crabtree was feeling sorry for several situations around him one afternoon, mostly about his mother, and started walking. He just wanted to be alone. He took his usual path through town, out Trail Road, past the Ranch entrance, and on by the motel. Mike was angry with God that his mother had a stroke and was now a vegetable, and that there just wasn't anything he could do to help her. He was also mad with his dad for deserting her – and him.

Mike likes to sit on the top edge of the canyon that runs under the viaduct and around the town. This is his place of solitude.

As he passed the motel, the door was apparently locked and it had a sign 'Be Back Soon' on it. The Motel Marquee read '*Rainrest Motel.*' He always thought that was a pretty apropos name for the motel with all the rain the mountain gets.

Mike usually has his trumpet and harmonica with him. He loves to blow the trumpet over the canyon and hear all the reverberations come back at him. It is almost like Heavenly Angels blowing their trumpets with him. A truly marvelous sound.

A young lady seems to enjoy the angel's trumpets too, because every time he visits the place she shows up as soon as she hears his trumpet. As he plays, her small figure will come and sit down on the top edge too; about a hundred-feet west of him, just close enough he can see the shadow of her face. He has noticed something unusual about her face.

She doesn't seem to want any company, so he leaves her alone. Mike has no idea where she comes from, or why she always seems so sad, and he has even witnessed her evidently wiping her tears on the tails of her blouse. He sometimes worries about her getting hurt, or a wild animal killing her. The young lady always stays there as long as he does.

When he sings into the canyon with his beautiful tenor voice, he believes he can see her jaws moving; that perhaps she might be singing with him, or just lip-sinking the words.

When he gets up to leave, she stands up too, but waits until he is gone before she goes back to wherever she is from.

He had decided to start praying for her safety - and frame of mind. He would be leaving for the Air Force two days after the wedding, and he wished he could get an address to write to her.

He decided to leave her a card telling her that.

The next time he went to his place of solitude, the card was gone, and there was a note saying: Donna – Box 28 – *Raincroft*. No last name, no physical address, nothing. But that was all right. He would write Box 28 with little tidbits of his adventures. He couldn't do anything for his mother, except send money back for her from the military, but perhaps he can help this young girl through her loneliness.

People were leaving the party. Almost everyone was gone – but - Todd and Kelli, they were still singing. Seems like they didn't know the party was over. The sparks flying between them were obvious to everyone around. Todd would just have to take her home and get Clarence's piano back to him any way he could. Good thing it's a Spinet with wheels. Jake had no doubt that Todd could handle that little job.

Clarence didn't seem to mind the wait; he was sitting in the shadows enjoying the music and watching love blossom, it felt good to an old man's heart to see life sprouting. Clarence had remained a widower since his lovely wife, Sarah, died over thirty-five years ago.

When Jake dropped Carrie off at home to spell her brother's mom-sitting, Mike already had his trumpet in hand and his harmonica in his pocket. He was going for a walk.

Mike would leave a note inviting Donna to the wedding. Jake noted the piece of paper in Mike's shirt pocket; he could see writing on it, but not what it said.

While making rounds in the woods Jake has heard Mike's trumpet blowing and his harmonica playing and his singing into the canyon, but knows he shouldn't intrude. Every man needs a place of solitude. Mike's is the North Canyon, and his is Blessing Pond. Hard decisions can be made in these quiet places. It's so revitalizing to spend time really alone with God.

Jake and Angela drove deeper into the woods where they could be alone for a short while. As he parked and hopped out of the ATV, his little red head stood up on her seat and stepped over into his seat - waiting for him to lift her out into his arms. He had gotten used to lifting her with just his right arm around her waist and pulling her to him. His left arm was still restricted in its cast.

"I think the surprise party went really well, don't you my love?" He asked her.

"Yea, an' 'specially since we wer' ther' together." She replied.

Jake told Angela about everything that had happened that day, and how he was extremely impressed with Sonny's observations and advice on 'the projects.' He also told her how he is now comfortable with how the young man will treat the ladies', and that Sonny wants to be like him.

His little red-head listened to Jake talk as she gazed into his eyes, and then decided she would rather smooch than listen right now, so she kissed her man warmly again and again. They spent about half an hour in the woods holding each other before he took her back to Orpha's, and headed for home.

Angela was talking to Mam on the phone every day, and sometimes two or three times a day. He had heard tid-bits, and Jake knew it had something to do with the vows they had made up. He had heard Angela practicing saying the alphabet as Mam said the letters to her. Mam's schooling with the guys was in full force, but since Angela had no way to get there, her schooling was by telephone.

Jess had taken off with Beth; they were just going to ride around for a while before he had to have her back at the ranch. First, they would visit Roscoe. Jess was still trying to get Beth to talk about the thing that puts her in 'space' – sometimes right in the middle of a conversation. Her grandpa was also trying to get her to open up, but whatever it was, it was not coming to light. Roscoe was delighted with how far she had come, and with the way Jess was being a gentleman around his grand-daughter.

"He's going to be a true-penny attorney, and fairly soon." Roscoe would say right out loud to himself quite often.

Todd and Kelli finally realized they were the only ones left at the party, other than Mr. Bloom. They grinned sheepishly at Clarence, and Todd rolled the piano back into the shop. He thanked

Clarence profusely for the use of it – and for not rushing he and Kelli. Mr. Bloom told Todd he was enjoying the beautiful music, and wasn't in any hurry at all to be alone again.

As they got into Todd's little Toyota he asked Kelli if she'd like something to eat off the Dollar Menu.

She chuckled, "Yes."

Todd kept studying her every feature as they ate; it made her a bit nervous.

"Why are you looking at me like that?" She finally asked him.

"Just because you are so good to look at." He responded grinning at her.

When Todd dropped Kelli off at her home, he walked her up on the porch and gave her a hug before he left. Kelli watched him as he was leaving; feeling happy inside; even though the thunder and lightning was starting again. She couldn't remember the last time they had so much lightning in a rainy season. The cracks of thunder shook the whole house.

Kelli knew Orpha would be scared, so she ran over to sit with Angela while she consoled her mother. She could remember how Manny Crabtree would hold Orpha during a storm, sometimes for hours. Kelli knew Manny still sneaks in once and a while to visit her – when he thinks no one is watching. Her heart goes out to both of them. Sometimes life just plain gives us lemons.

Informing the Boys & Ira's Heartache

When Wiley stopped the Jeep at Annabelle's he sat quietly for a bit. The rain was coming down at a pretty good clip and the thunder and lightning were really cracking. Wiley grabbed the blanket out of the back seat and put it over Annabelle as they all ran into the house. Wayne could feel something bothering Wiley, because the big man hadn't said much on the way home.

After everyone had removed their muddy shoes, and they were drying themselves off, Wayne finally asked Wiley, "Are you OK?"

"Yes, son, I just have something heavy on my mind and heart – and - I need to talk to both of you boys about it." Wiley said slowly.

The boys were both all ears, Wiley's usual up beat countenance was almost gloomy, and they were both asking why.

"Let's sit down for a bit so I can talk to you." Wiley told them.

"I'll make drinks." Annabelle commented as Wiley and the two boys sat down at the kitchen table.

Wiley started talking softly. "I want you both to know that I know very well what you both went through watching your father waste away and die from *Sickle Cell Disease*. You see, my father died of the disease just as I turned sixteen years old. I had taken care of him for many years all by myself. My mother died when I was four years old, while having my sister, who died with her. My dad and I were alone for the rest of the time. So, I very much know what you boys went through. You don't have to say anything; I just want you to know I do know how terrible your father's death was for each of you.

I care very much for you both, and for your mother. I would take you as my sons even without her; I've come to love you for who you are, not just because of your wonderful mother. I've been very lonely since my father died, and I've done a lot of praying for a family of my own. My prayers now are for you three to be my family. I know I cannot take the place of your birth father, but I would be grateful to be your step-father and protector."

Wiley was in tears by now, so was Annabelle. The boys were also fighting them back.

"What if we have the disease, Wiley?" Wayne asked point blank.

"Wayne," Wiley answered, "we'll cross that bridge if and when we need to. But I promise you I will not desert you if you do. I will care for you and your mother through whatever comes our way. After waiting so many years for a family, I won't run. Please think about what I have told you. I would never get deeply involved with your mother without both of you approving; even if it takes another ten years. I will never take her away from you nor let her or you go through anything bad again all alone."

Neither boy said anything. They looked at each other, then excused themselves and went to their bedroom. Wiley's words really needed digesting, and they would have to talk about the possibilities. As soon as they left the room the crying Annabelle and Wiley held each other close for several minutes. He would wait until the noisy atmosphere quieted down before he left; he is now fully aware of how much afraid of storms this lady is.

He was praying as he drove that God wouldn't let his words drive a wedge between himself and the boys.

As Ira's old red Dodge pulled into The Equine Trails Dude Ranch, Ira was feeling a big loss; and when he looked over at Leslie he felt she was feeling one also.

"Well, what time will you be leaving Saturday morning?" Ira asked her.

"Probably about five o'clock. It's a long drive and I'll probably stay in a motel about half way home." She responded.

"Are you sure you can drive that far without re-injuring your foot? I can drive you and then fly back: Jake will pick me up in the City." Ira suggested.

"I'll be all right – I'm kind of going to miss being cradled like a baby, but I have to get back to being an aggressive and authoritative agent. Back to solving crimes." Leslie told him.

"You could always move back here to *Raincroft* and help your parents with the Ranch. They're expanding you know, and will need more help." Ira insisted.

"I know, but I have a degree in Forensic Investigation, and I love my job." She insisted back.

The two sat quietly watching the rainfall - and each other - before Ira spoke again, "When will you be back again?"

"Well, next time I come in I'll fly, and someone can pick me up at City Airport. I'm going to try to be back in about six months; I know mom and dad are getting older – and I need to spend time with them."

"I'll pick you up anywhere," Ira assured her, "just let me know the time and place."

He had a glimmer that her needing to spend time with her parents might also include someone else – like him?

"Can we go to dinner tomorrow night?" He inquired.

"Well, since it's Wednesday night, there is church: but after that we can have a late dinner. OK?" She asked.

He wasn't too keen on going to church, but he would certainly make an exception. "Must I meet you there, or will I be able to pick you up?" He asked her.

"You can pick me up about six-thirty if that's all right." She replied.

"Absolutely perfect." He responded, as his heart lifted a bit.

When the rain broke to just a few drops, Ira carried Leslie to the door and inside where he sat her down on a dining room chair.

He gave her a peck on her cheek – and left.

The big man had not really been actively pursuing an accounting course, but now that Todd has a computer, and Mam said she would teach him, he'd better get with the program. He really needs a better education – and a better paying job. Ira has been amazed at how fast his brother picked up the computer all on his own, sort of like a duck takes to water. He's made numerous calls to Josie, and seems to comprehend everything she says to him. Mam is pleased with Todd's progress.

Leslie sat there for several moments before her Mom came into the room and sat down beside her and said, "Deep in thought, Honey? Want to talk about something? Perhaps a mountain man?"

"Mom, Ira's so uncouth and uneducated, and we live so far away from each other, that starting any kind of a relationship with him is out of the question. Besides, I love my job. No, I have to keep things platonic; Ira and I have no future together, just too many uncorrectable variables." Leslie assured her mother.

Emily sighed heavily before she spoke, "You know, Honey, the Lord does work in mysterious ways. Most things have a way of working out – but you cannot be unequally yoked – and Ira's not a Christian. That's the biggest stumbling block."

"He's picking me up for church tomorrow night, and then we'll go to dinner." Leslie told her mom.

"Well, Honey, that's a start – but there's a long way to go before he is ready to commit to the Lord," Emily resounded, "but just think, Todd has been coming to church on Sunday for several weeks now, and we've noticed significant change in his attitude. At first your dad and I thought it was just to be close to Kelli, but we're watching his heart soften and his real interest in what your dad is saying. God is still in the business of miracles."

"Jake has been talking to Ira about the Lord, and to Sonny for a long time, I don't know how many of Jake's words have stuck," Leslie confessed, "but I have witnessed an attitude change in Ira. He doesn't use the foul language, and he doesn't smoke now. So, something must be getting through. Down in the canyon Jake talked quite a bit to Sonny, and I could tell Ira was taking it all in…I think I will write to Ira though."

MARIE GRACE

Father – Son Advice & A Sad Good Bye

Dad's little metallic turquoise project in the garage was coming along really nicely; it would be finished in plenty of time before the wedding. You would not believe that it is the same little vehicle that he and Lester Craddock slid from Lester's pick up into the GMC. Dad told Jake that he and Ira could take it to the City in just a couple of days to get it street licensed in Jake's name.

Dad had mounted some wide wheels and tires on it, and large magnets in the rims to hug the magnet strips dad had put in the path. He had put in a geared down transmission so it could safely maneuver to Orpha's home and around the woods. The roll bars were even painted the turquoise metallic. Mam had made some cushions with backs – to help keep her grandkid's mother from jiggling around too much.

Of course, Little Joe had put a camera on it in case his new sister got into trouble. John and Josie would be giving the little vehicle to their new little daughter for a wedding gift – before the wedding. Both were kind of hoping that Angela, Kelli and Carrie would arrive at the wedding in it – it would make some wonderful pictures - if Angela learns how to drive it by whenever IT is.

Jake was sure he could teach her pretty fast, "She's more up on 'things' than I first thought," he said to his father, "– where'd she learned to tease me?"

Dad snickered, "It's in her genes."

As dad and Jake worked together in the basement, John was trying to counsel him on how to treat his new wife, "If you are rough with her at first, she'll become frigid, so my most important advice to you is to be gentle in all things. According to *Hebrews 13:4, (KJV) 'The marriage bed is undefiled.'* However, Son, that means if everything is consensual and non-injurious."

His dad went on, "Always remember her heart rules her, which is the way God made her. Another thing to always bear in mind – women have very - very - long memories, and if you hurt them that hurt can sometimes last for many years. Always consider her feelings before yours. YOU are responsible for the countenance others will see in her.

"If she turns cold, it is because you were uncaring or clumsy, and it's very hard to thaw a hurt woman. Talk with her often and see how she feels about things, she has as much right to her feelings as you do, just remember there is no right or wrong to feelings.

"Another thing to keep in mind, she is your wife, not your 'property.' Let her remain true to herself. You fell in love with Angela like she is, don't try to change her. You have no right to badger her or push her around; reminding people of things is a sign of disrespect. You ask her opinion; you don't give her orders: just suggestions for her to think about.

"I know you will never lay a hand on her, but I need to say this anyway – never, never, ever, lay a violent hand on her - or any object. Any thought of violence toward her will incite not only the wrath of God on you – but also your mother's and mine. We'll skin you within an inch of your life.

"Anyone you hear degrading her deserves your knuckle sandwich.

"Your mother and I have a wonderful marriage, and we are still great lovers, and we want that for you too. The primary reason our marriage is so strong is because I have followed what I just told you. I know your great heart, son, and your mother and I know you will follow our examples – however, your Mom is the only one allowed to take the broom handle to you."

Jake and his dad were both crying as they hugged each

other. The big man knew deep in his heart that he was one of the most favored men in the entire earth with Josie and John Judd as his parents. He gave his father the solemn promise that he would follow their example – and his words.

"Now," Dad continued, "With both of us working, let's see if we can finish this metallic tank this evening, then perhaps we can give it to her Friday afternoon, just before your romantic dinner."

Jake looked down at the heavy-duty bumpers dad had put on both ends, he was sure they were his mother's idea – protecting the mother of her grandkids. Dad had installed the seat belts on his own in both the front and rear. He too was thinking of his grandkid's safety. Both John and Josie are really looking forward to being grandparents, and they both promised to spoil them…that's their job.

About ten that night, dad and Jake loaded the adorable little vehicle on the pull trailer. It was too tall with the roll bars to fit in the back of the GMC. It had solar batteries that would run for at least eight hours on one charge, and if it was in the sun it would run continuously. Plus, dad had hooked up a small gas engine back-up that would start automatically if the solar batteries got low.

The families' little red head would be all right.

Jake called Ira and asked him if he could take a trip in the morning to the City to register the little tank. Ira was very happy to go with him, so Jake told Ira he would be picking him up about eight. Dad would be taking the ATV to work. John always liked to drive the ATV; it almost made him feel like a youngster again.

On the way to the City Ira was telling Jake about how he was going to miss Leslie; he had really enjoyed having her around, but he knew the possibility of them being together was pretty farfetched.

"She is pretty, educated and upper class, and I'm just a scruffy dumb old mountain man." Ira told Jake.

"Well, scruffy yes, dumb no," Jake came back, "you might need some education, but you're not at all dumb. You still planning on getting some accounting courses? I understand that Lenore Patton is looking forward to retiring in a couple of years; she wants to move to Albuquerque to be close to her widowed daughter and two grandkids. Since she's the only accountant in town, perhaps you might think about getting better acquainted with her."

"I didn't know Lenore was about to retire," Ira responded, "do you think she might actually help me to become an accountant? I don't have any money to pay her for her business; I wonder if she would take a Contract and sixty percent of the profits for the first two years, if I approached her right. I wonder how much rent she pays for her office? Or maybe she owns the building."

Ira's mind was going crazy.

"You can't know unless you ask." Jake assured him, realizing Ira's mind was already running figures.

Ira had trimmed his beard and combed it neatly, along with making sure his nails were clean and filed, and he used mouth wash after brushing his teeth until his gums started bleeding. He put stinky on. Not only was he going to church, he was taking Leslie out for a late dinner. The last one they would be sharing because she was leaving early Saturday morning.

Ira had even washed, waxed and vacuumed his old vehicle.

It looked like she too had put extra effort into looking nice tonight. She knew Ira loves ladies in pink, so she had on a pink pantsuit. He told her how lovely she looked as he closed his truck door after setting her in place, then he laid her crutches in the back of the pickup.

In church her father, John Stoddard, was preaching on fulfilling what God has for you to do. Some of his words were akin to Jakes. Ira could feel a stirring in his guts and wasn't aware what it was. Ira was glad when the service was over; he didn't like unusual feelings…unless they involved Leslie.

Ira took Leslie to the *Canyon Steak Corral.* Being the middle of the week it was almost empty, and that was great as far as Ira was concerned. They walked over to the round corner booth, and each slid in one side.

Ernie Caldwell was their waiter and welcomed them as he

handed them menus, "Welcome to the *Canyon Steak Corral*, can I get you something from the bar?"

"No," Leslie replied for both of them, "just coffee and water."

I would have ordered a glass of dark wine. Ira thought to himself.

But then Leslie commented, "I don't need any liquor when I'm with good company."

Ira no longer wanted any alcohol.

"Ira," Leslie continued, "your verbiage seems to have improved since I last talked to you. Any particular reason?"

"You know your dad got Todd a computer? Well Todd, Billy and I have been studying English together with the free encyclopedia. It's been fun practicing speaking properly to each other, almost like a game. I've also been schooling with Josie. Noticeable, huh?" Ira answered a question with a question.

"It is." She replied.

They decided what they would order to eat, and gave the orders to Ernie, who noticed there was never a lull in their conversation.

"So, what do you want to be when you grow up?" Leslie asked Ira point blank. He wasn't sure if she was just teasing or meant business. After all, she is an Investigator and right on questions are part of her job.

"On the way to the City this morning," Ira related, "Jake was telling me that Lenore Patton is planning on retiring in a couple of years. I don't know if she would be willing to take me on or not. I'd love to buy her business, but I don't have any money. You know us Carson boys have always just gotten by – by the skin of our teeth. We're not trained in anything. We just do what we have to do to get things done."

"Poppycock." Leslie replied to what he thought was an honest answer.

"Come again -." Ira objected.

"You can do anything you want to, Ira Carson. You're not a dummy, I was in school with you, remember? You'd ace a math test without even studying. How do you know you can't come to some type of an agreement if you don't even try? You're lacking in English, but that's certainly correctable." Leslie was point blank.

"Man, you don't mince words, do you?" Ira expressed his observation.

"Nope." She affirmed.

"Maybe I'll just go see Lenora and try and talk with her." Ira fired back.

"Good idea, nothing ventured – nothing gained. She can't do anything but say "yes" or "no", so you have nothing to lose. Besides, I'm going to be praying that God will open up a door for you." Leslie informed Ira.

Ira shook his head in agreement – albeit doubting that God would do anything for him.

Talk turned to the lighter side as they started recalling things they had done together the last two weeks, and how he had carried her everywhere – even though she had mastered the crutches.

The ticklebug hit them, and they were laughing at everything. The sweat rings the cold glasses were making were even funny; they'd run their fingers through the rings and try to pick an image out of the moisture. Ira was glad she had such a good sense of humor under that gruff surface – kinda like him. They had both slid closer to the back of the booth – toward each other.

She told him that tomorrow evening was going to be family time, and Friday she would be packing and talking with the home office to get caught up on several situations she had been working on. This was the last time they would see each other until the next time she came to town.

"Hopefully I'll be back in about six months for a visit." She reminded him.

"At least that's something to look forward to." Ira responded.

When he picked her up to leave the restaurant about eleven, no one even paid any attention. Everyone had grown accustomed to this as a norm. As he sat her in the pick-up, he paused a few seconds before he released his grip on her. She didn't seem to be trying to get away. They were both silent on the drive back to the Ranch.

"Will you write to me, Leslie?" He asked her as he pulled in and parked.

"Yes, I will." She informed him positively.

John and Emily were sitting on the front porch, so Ira knew he probably should place her in one of the chairs beside them and say his good bye. He reached in the back of the truck and retrieved her crutches, handed them to her to hang on to, and picked her up.

He hadn't even sat her down on the porch beside her parents before a great loss filled his heart again.

A Surprise Gift & A Romantic Dinner

Jake was so excited when he pulled into Angela's. There were several surprises waiting for her. The first one in the basement with the family. The next in their own apartment having dinner – all alone.

Not only had Mam prepared Lasagna, honey rolls and salads, she had dug out a pair of antique candlestick holders and put a candle in each one, with a book of matches beside them. The ceramic candleholders were roses with mint green leaves, they had been her mothers. Jani found two white sparkly candles to fit them at the Nielsen Market.

Josie put three antique lace placemats on the table, one for under each place setting, and one in the center to put the candlesticks on. She had run the dishwasher to be sure the dishes Angela had picked out were clean and ready to use. Mam set the table with their new dishes, ready for food. The glasses were upside down to keep any dust out of them, and she had put some of her fancy paper napkins beside each plate. The table really looked beautiful.

Mam had also made a jug of raspberry ice tea and put it in the refrigerator. Josie and Jani made the bed up with the clean new linens, and even hung the towels in the bathroom. Then when they left –they locked the tunnel door behind them. The night was all set.

The family could all be present when dad presented her with her wedding gift, but everyone was barred from the apartment. Her turquoise tank was all street legal, and Jake had ordered the special license plate saying 'My Red'. The special plate will take a few days to get there, but it would arrive in plenty time for the wedding. There was a cardboard temporary license plate that showed the permanent one had been ordered.

Jake had told the family that he would have his soon-to-be-wife there about four thirty, so everyone was waiting when the ATV came down the elevator. Angela knew immediately something was up – and it must be good because everyone was smiling big.

Mam was the first to give her a big hug, then Dad, Jani and the rest of the family. Angela noticed the big hump sitting in the middle of the floor covered with a blue plastic tarp. Jani had her digital, and so did Jess. Uncle Ernie was in his usual white lab coat and green mesh hairnet; half jumping with excitement.

"Angela," dad began, "we are all so happy that you are now a part of our family. We also know you will have to keep watch over your mother every day, and need your own transportation to get back and forth. Even though you don't have your driver's license yet, Sheriff Leo said you could drive this for a short time as long as we have insurance on it, and accept all responsibility. We do have full coverage insurance on it, and I have told the sheriff I accept full responsibility for any damage at all. The papers are in the glove box."

And with that he pulled the cover off the little turquoise tank.

Jake's little red head was flabbergasted as the whole family walked her over to her new wheels. Angela walked around it, and kept touching it all over.

"Cain I get in it?" She asked dad.

"Sure, it's yours." Dad assured her.

As she scooted in behind the wheel and sat down, Jake got in the rider's seat. He smiled as he said to her, "Now, here's how you drive your little tank. This is the key, you just put it in that slot, and turn it to the right. The big pedal on the floor is the brake, and the small one is the foot-feed to make your tank move. This is the 'shifter' handle that you use to move your gear-shift to go forward or backwards, and if you are just sitting still and talking to someone you put the arrow here on the N for neutral. You just press this black button on the top of this shifter and that releases it to move to where you want it.."

The big man pointed to everything as he explained each item to her. This F on the handle stands for forward and the R is for reverse.

"Tha's easy to remember." She exclaimed.

He explained it has solar batteries, with a gasoline back up, and that Little Joe had put a camera on it that would keep her safe. He showed her how to turn the camera on and off, how to turn the lights on and use the turning signals, and work the windshield wipers.

"Jus' like a real car." Angela said gleefully.

Dad showed her how to unroll the canvas on top of the bars in case it started to rain, or the sun got too hot, and tie the two front corner straps to the front roll bar and the back two corner straps to the back roll-bar to keep the canvas in place. John had also put a plastic 'trunk' on the back to carry supplies in, and still be lightweight.

Mam gave her the 'garage door opener'; it was all programmed for her. As she punched a button, the top of the elevator got real light from the sun for five seconds, and then went back dark, so she punched it a second time. There came the light again.

"It works," she exclaimed, "cain we take my tank for a ride?"

"Sure," dad cut in, "you and Jake take it for a spin, and we'll go back about our business, and leave you two alone for the rest of the evening."

The turquoise tank jerked a couple of times as she stepped on the foot feed, but after a few trips around the garage, she had the gas pedal smoothed out and was moving the cart slowly to the elevator. She was jumping up and down on the seat - as much as the belts would allow her to move. Jake pushed the button to bring the elevator down from its upper level resting place.

When she pulled onto the elevator, she put the arrow on the gear shift handle on the N. Jake pushed the elevator button, and it started up. At the top when the rock moved after she pushed the button, she stepped down too hard on the pedal, and the cart bolted off the elevator.

Jake hit the brake, and after he caught his wind he told her, "Easy baby, you have to come slowly off the elevator or you'll go over the edge. The rock won't hit you. Little Joe put a sensor in the rock and if something is in its view, it won't close but will go back up. Now you want to hug the mountain as you slowly go down the path."

Angela knew what slowly was now, and she was creeping along. Jake was not going to tell her to go any faster, she'd figure out a safe speed all by herself. She was really doing well, and the big man was proud of his little woman. Just because she is 'back woods' doesn't mean she is dumb. She's actually very bright.

When she got to the turn-around she put the cart in the N (neutral) again, took a few big breaths of relief. She made sure the camera was off before she grabbed her man and kissed him firmly.

They sat there in N for several minutes just enjoying each other before Jake asked her; "Do you want to drive to your mom's?"

Angela answered by putting the cart in F and pushing down on the little pedal; she was ready to go anywhere. Jake wanted to be sure she was able to maneuver the ruts in the path leading to Orpha's.

As they pulled up into the driveway everyone came running out. Angela hadn't had one single problem driving her turquoise tank.

"Do you want to call Mam and let her know how good you did?" Jake suggested.

Angela was pushing Josie's green button before Jake had finished his sentence, "Hi Josie Judd, this is Angela Crabtree, and we didn't have any problems at all getting here. Jake said I'm really good."

She hadn't told Mam where they had made it to, but she had a pretty good idea, she could hear all the chatter in the background.

Everyone wanted a ride. Angela wanted Carrie and Kelli to ride first so they jumped in the back.

"Fas'en yur seat belts before we cain take off." Angela ordered.

The little red head drove them around for about fifteen minutes, and then she took Pam and Will for the same fifteen-minute drive around the woods. The entire woods were filled with excitement as everyone was laughing and hollering at neighbors.

Angela's brother, Mike, wasn't home so he would get a ride later.

Jake wheeled Orpha out on the porch so she could see Angela's wheels, and her arm started going crazy, she loved the little turquoise tank.

They tried to get Nellie to take a ride, but unless Walter is home, she will not come out of the house.

After everyone around had a ride, Jake and Angela started the trip back up the path and into the garage. When they reached the turn-around Angela let up off the foot pedal and slowed down to the crawl speed again, and took off up the mountain. She called ahead to be sure no one was headed down the mountain path as she had been told to do. There certainly wasn't room for two vehicles to pass. The little red head didn't have a single problem.

She pushed the button on her remote and the big rock rolled back. She drove straight into the elevator and put the tank in N as Jake pushed the elevator's down button. Angela then turned to Jake and pulled his head over to hers so she could kiss her wonderful man. Too bad the elevator didn't take longer to get down - but they would be alone for their dinner.

When the elevator stopped she pulled off of it like a pro and drove over to the spot John had parked it. She turned off the key and waited for Jake to get her door. Then she grabbed the blue plastic tarp to cover her little bug so it wouldn't get dusty. Hand in hand they headed through the garden, and up the stairs.

The door at the top was shut. Jake scooped his beloved up in his arms, and asked her to open the door. When she did she could see their living room furniture all in place. He carried her all around the apartment – after he had shut and Angela locked the door behind them. He showed her the finished bathroom – and then the bedroom.

It looked beautiful; all made up with the linens. Jake dropped her on the bed.

"How does that feel?" He asked her.

"Like I nev'r want ta leav'." She answered as she grabbed him and pulled him down on the bed too.

Sparks were flying as they lay there holding each other close, gently rubbing each other's backs amid long sweet kisses and embraces. She had said it well, he nev'r wanted ta leav' either. This is going to be his wife, and her inviting love is almost too much to handle.

"We have to look at the kitchen," he finally said, "Mam has a surprise for us."

Angela wasn't too quick to turn loose of him – even for a surprise.

The little red head was in awe at how beautiful their home was; she was running her fingers over everything.

As they walked into the kitchen, there was the table all set fancy. Jake had put the table by the patio windows so they could look out at the beautiful scenery as they ate.

He lit the candles as soon as he could unglue her and help her sit down. By the time he got to the oven to turn it on – she was glued to him again. He took the pan of lasagna out of the refrigerator and put it in the oven – then asked her if she would please put out the salads and drinks. The honey rolls were in aluminum foil ready to be put in the oven for about three minutes when the lasagna had finished heating.

She sat the salads on the table and filled the glasses with ice from her new icemaker, making them overflow. Angela was having so much fun with the icemaker they were playing ice cube pick up. Jake poured the tea into the glasses and handed her one as he headed for the patio.

They stood looking at the National Geographic scene, holding each other tight amid kisses, until the buzzer went off.

"That's the stove my love," he told her, "the lasagna is done and we can put the rolls in for three minutes."

She followed him to the stove, and he looked for something

to grab the hot pan with. There were no hot pads, so she found two dishcloths in a drawer and gave them to him to use as hot pads. He sat the dish on top of the stove and stuck the rolls in the oven.

"Now, my sweet, let's eat our first meal in our new home." He grinned as he bowed his head to say grace after they sat down at the table.

As they started eating their salads, both were cooing. Buzz, the rolls were hot, and the lasagna should be set up by now, so Jake went to get the vittles. Angela put a folded-up dishtowel on the table to protect it from the hot pans, even though it is Formica.

Mam had put a big spatula on the stove to serve the hot food with – and was Jake glad. He would also be glad when he got that darned cast off in two more weeks.

"Well, my lovely lady," Jake said softly, we need to set a date for our wedding, I think three weeks would be good for me because my cast will be off and I will have had time to exercise my arm back to good shape. What do you think?"

"Well, Jakie," she cooed, if we cain't be married tonight, I guess three weeks is ok. Then I won' 'ave to stop teasin' ya anymore."

The big man could feel his temperature going up quick, so he retrieved some three by five-file cards and a pen out of a drawer he had put them in to get the subject changed.

"How does Saturday the fifteenth of June sound to you? About eleven o'clock so we won't get so tired with a big long day." He asked his little bombshell.

"Yesss, I cain be a June bride." She loved the idea of the fifteenth. "Now, we need to make plans. We have to plan for flowers, the cake and punch, tuxedos, nuts, mints, coffee and tea…"

She was going on and on. Jake was trying to write the subject on top of each file card as she blurted it out.

Angela knew about all the fixings for a wedding, she had been studying, "Kelli an' me got a bride book at the Do Over an' been lookin' at the pictures. Maybe she can use the bride book when she an' Todd get married."

"You're pretty sure she and Todd will be married?" He asked his little woman.

"Yep, we've been prayin', jus' like I did for yu, an when he sees her in her gown he'll go bonkers." She assured him.

They made lots of lists on the cards. When everything they could think of was listed, he put the cards in his pocket. Angela didn't have a pocket, but she told him he could put them in her bra. He shook his head no and started taking the dishes to the sink, and put the leftovers in the refrigerator.

She helped him load her new dishwasher, and even though there was hardly anything in it she had to run it. Mam had left her some Cascade Complete.

"I jus' luv my new mom," she told Jake, "she takes care of me."

Jake was realizing more and more that the 'little things', like Josie leaving her dishwasher detergent, touches her heart more than a big thing. He must always remember that.

Jake walked her back out to the patio; he wanted to avoid the bedroom. They sat down in their settee and watched as the sun was setting and things were glowing different colors. The waves in the lake below were so vibrant with sunrays that they could see their twinkles from their eagle's view. It wasn't a large pond, but a tributary from the river that circles *Raincroft*. Jake had watched wildlife come for a drink, especially in the evenings as he rested from his toil.

"Almost as beautiful as you," Jake told his love as she squiggled again in his arms, "this is so right, so wonderful, God gave you to me."

"An' yu ta me." She replied as their lips met again.

How good it was to hold each other, but their kissing and holding might be getting out of hand, because she was breathing in his ear again.

"Shall we go tell Mom and Dad about the date so they will be the first to know?" He asked her softly.

She paused before she agreed, "Yea, I want them to be th' firs' ta' know our weddin' date."

He kissed her a few more long sweet kisses before he stood her up and took her hand to head for Mam's kitchen - and safety.

Good thing her lean frame didn't weigh too much, because peeling her off of him was getting harder, both because she didn't want to let him go – and because he certainly didn't want to let her go.

Mam heard them coming down the hall. The whole family was sitting around the kitchen obviously waiting for news.

Angela ran over and hugged Mam, "Guess wha? We're gettin' married on June fifteenth, I'll be a June bride."

Josie, Jani and Angela were jumping around like little bunny rabbits with excitement. The men did some hugs, but light ones; mostly their excitement was by way of handshakes – chest bumps - and watching the gleeful ladies...

Dad gave Angela a big hug as he told her, "I understand you were a terrific driver with your new wheels - good job."

Jake would follow her home since it was dark out now, and there's nothing going to harm his sweet little lady.

More Wedding Plans & A Black Truck

By morning the whole town knew the wedding date. Angela was driving her turquoise tank everywhere, and giving rides. Dad Judd had witnessed her putting lots of miles on the little cart, and when she was parked at Nielsen's he walked over and told her to stop by *The Grease Pod* so he could fill the gas tank. Dad didn't know if the auto-switch had transferred the engine to the gas backup or not, but he didn't want to take a chance on his new daughter running out of power since the clouds were forming again overhead.

When she pulled in to the station, she jumped out and gave Dad a big hug. Angela was really flying high with excitement.

"I think it'd be cute fur us girls to rid' to the weddin' in this, don' yu?" She asked Dad.

"Sounds like a good idea to me, it would be great for pictures." Dad agreed with her. *Josie's wish is coming true,* dad was thinking to himself.

"Good, then we'll do it." She responded. It didn't take her long to decide.

Jake and Angela made a trip to *The Floristic*. Pam was working that day and really happy to help them with their flower order...and to know the date of the wedding. They needed a cascading bride's bouquet: and they wanted white roses, both full sized and miniature, along with green carnations and white Baby's

Breath. On her bridal bouquet Angela wanted big bows made of the white and mint green ribbons with tails that would reach almost to the ground.

Pam thought the colors sounded beautiful. The bridesmaid, Kelli, will also get a smaller cascading bouquet to match Angela's. Both mothers' corsages would be white roses and green carnations, with powder blue ribbon on Josie's, and mint green ribbon on Orpha's. Jani's corsage ribbon would also be mint green. They couldn't say what color Carrie and Pam's ribbons would be until they picked out their dresses, so they decided on white to be safe.

Emily, Mia and Beth will also have white ribbon since Angela didn't know what they would be wearing to coordinate the reception.

The shop also had a really pretty white satin guest book in the glass case, and they sure need that. Pam said she could decorate it with miniature mint green ribbon and roses, and add some baby's breath and sequin their names and wedding date on it. Jake and Angela thought that sounded fantastic.

Angela didn't suppose they'd remember who all was there at the ceremony, and they could read the names later. Besides she said when they open their gifts Kelli can just list the gift by the name in the Guest Book and won't have to rewrite the names. Pam thought that was an excellent idea, lists get so messy and lost so fast. The Guest Book would be perfect.

The more Jake watched and listened to his soon-to-be wife, the more impressed he was becoming; she did seem to have everything under control.

Jake will wear a full size white rose and mint carnation. The men's boutonnieres will be miniature white roses & mint carnations. Angela was planning out loud; they will need ones for Jess, Dad John, Pastor John, Mike, Will, Todd, Little Joe, Barstow, Uncle Ernie, and Billy, along with Ira who will be picking up the flowers and helping Sarah bring the cakes and mints. Oh yes, they will also need one for Sarah, that'd only be right.

Unc was being assigned to the Guest Book, - and Ira was being assigned to Uncle Ernie, to be sure he doesn't disappear.

Jake had asked Ira if he wanted to sit up front with Mam and Dad and the rest of the family, but he said no: he wasn't ready to be that close to the front of a church yet.

As Jake paid for the flowers, Angela remarked, "Good thin' Pam gets a discoun', that'll save us a bunch o' money."

The big man was proud of his little lady counting the cost as he thought - *that's what the Bible tells us to do*. His heart also felt happy because she had called his dad –Dad John.

Jake would be wearing a white tuxedo with a mint bow tie and cummerbund. He has to get some new dress shoes. Since *Raincroft* has no rental store, the eight guys needing the forest green tuxedos, white shirts and mint ties, needed to put a time together when they could all go to the City. After checking with everyone, they could all go the following Tuesday. Jake called ahead for an appointment for the nine men about ten o'clock at the *Tux Rentals* shop.

Dad Judd would take Jake, Joe and Uncle Ernie in his King Cab GMC. Pastor John would take Jess, Will, Todd and Mike in his blue Ford one-ton Club Cab. They could go to *The Sweet Dragon* for lunch when they got finished with their measurements.

Barstow, Ira, Todd and Billy would be making a trip to the City in Barstow's truck to get plain dark navy suits. They didn't need tuxedos. Ira, Todd and Billy had never owned such a thing as a suit, but since Mam had given the orders, and the money, they had no choice. They even had to get new 'regular' shoes. Todd was strangely compliant, like he was looking forward to being all gussied up. In fact, Todd even wanted a bow tie. Billy seemed okay with dressing up; he is usually pretty easy to get along with – unless he gets really mad – then look out – he IS a Carson. It was Ira who was fussing. And ties? Ira had never had a tie on – and wasn't sure he was even going to wear one – but Mam's broom flashed through his mind – would she really use it on him? Jake said she would.

Barstow had several suits, but the knees were wearing thin and shiny, especially his navy suit. So, he decided to get with the program and get a new suit too. Besides he had to be sure the fellas got what they were supposed to. That didn't include new cowboy or engineer boots! He would also take them to *The Sweet Dragon* when they were done so they could empty the food counters. Good thing he has a Club Cab for all those legs.

Next Jake and Angela visited Sarah at *The Sweet Tooth*, and she and Angela discussed every single cake in her bridal book. Jake's little red head often liked to check out all possibilities before making a decision, and this was one of those times.

Every time she would ask Jake's opinion, he would just say, "Whatever you want sweetie."

They finally decided on a four level all-white cake with white butter frosting, and lots of white roses, mint green carnations, and dark green leaves. There would be four strands of Australian draped rope piping at three-inch intervals. The top-level would be elevated on pillars.

On top is an arch with white roses and doves clear across it and the bride and groom are standing under it. The arch and bride and groom are all porcelain to keep for many years. The plastic pillars are embossed with white ivy vines from bottom to top and rose ropes surround the bottom of the posts. There are a few mint green leaves woven into the Australian drapes laced around each layer, and white miniature roses that frame the bottom edge of each layer.

They also ordered four sheet cakes to feed about one hundred each, and they will be decorated to match the big cake; each piece to have a white rose and a green leaf. Angela asked Sarah to pre-cut the individual pieces in the sheet cakes.

Ira would be picking up the cakes about nine o'clock in the morning. Sarah will have them frozen so they won't dry out during the ceremony. She will provide a box especially for the top tier. Jake didn't know that they would freeze and eat the top layer on their first anniversary – but Angela did.

Sarah volunteered to go with Ira to set up the cakes at church. Sarah Deines has been sweet on Ira since high school, but rarely gets an opportunity to fellowship with him. She was a book-worm during school, and her most exciting thing was working part time at The Sweet Tooth, saving her money – and eventually buying the store from Randy Long when he retired three years ago.

With her mother passing away when she was young, Sarah became an introvert. Her thin five-foot-ten-inch frame could be seen watching people around the town from a park bench or out her store's front window. The ladies' congregating at the Gossipmark often wondered how she stayed so thin, about one-hundred-thirty pounds, working in a shop filled with delectable calories. They would snicker at how she seemed to tower above most of the town's ladies and a lot of the men. With her jet-black hair and dark brown eyes, they sometimes cruelly called her an over-ripe Beanpole: but even the gossips had to admit she did some of the finest work they had ever seen on pastries.

Jake and Angela would order their paper products through Maxine Vince at the *Hallmark Store*. Since Maxine was one of the gossips, they knew the wedding news would make it around the entire town by evening.

The fancy plates, napkins and glasses would take about ten days to get here, so they had to turn in an order right away. Of course, Angela had to look at all possibilities. She and Jake finally settled on a pattern that had the bridal bells superimposed over the cross of our Lord. They ordered complete services for five hundred guests.

It was just assumed that the whole town was invited. The couple had been making up flyers to post around town inviting everyone – Maxine is almost better than flyers.

Now for the photographer. Memories Photography Studio is right across from the *Town Square*. They popped in; not being sure what poses they wanted. Cindy Allen has owned the studio for many years; and is well-seasoned in wedding photography.

Although she likes to do the photos before the wedding, Jake said, "No. The photos of our wedding will be taken when we are married. If people don't want to wait they can leave."

Cindy would give them a list of each pose she would be taking, and they could inform everyone in advance; and that will cut down time. Memories Photography has several packages. Jake and his soon-to-be-wife looked through all of the packages and discussed them. The one that caught their eyes is the one that takes pictures from the arrival to the departure, the dressing rooms, sanctuary, kitchen and everything, plus it includes photos of the rehearsal and dinner. Cindy has an assistant that will be helping her so they don't miss anything. It has over three-hundred-fifty pictures in the package called *'Remembrance,'* and that's the one they chose.

They know many people will have cameras and camcorders with them, but they want an official record. The package also comes with a beautiful white bridal album, and since they already have their album, Angela said they could give it to Kelli for her hope chest; she and Todd will need it when they get married.

It was a pretty expensive package; but Jake has never heard a bad comment on Cindy's work. Cindy also will be setting up three stationary video cameras; one in the back of the sanctuary and one in the front stationed on the bride and groom. The third one will be on the head table at the reception. Plus, Cindy will have an extra portable video camera and will move about the festivities with it.

The rehearsal dinner and reception would be held in the basement kitchen and dining room of the church. The basement facilities will hold about two-hundred-fifty people. If too many show up for the reception, they will just have to eat where ever they can find a seat – or stand. The kitchen is already stocked with 2 sixty-five-cup percolators, one they use for regular coffee and one for decaf, ice tea urns and several beverage pitchers.

John Judd contacted Eva and Ernie Caldwell of the *Canyon Steak Corral* to cater the rehearsal dinner for thirty-five; making a couple extra meals, in case someone showed up unexpectedly. Mam offered to fix the banquet, but John had told her definitely not, she just doesn't need that much work added with everything else going on. Any excess food would go in containers and put in Jake and Angela's freezer for them to thaw and eat later.

The rehearsal was scheduled for six o'clock Thursday night, but Pastor John asked Jake and Angela to be at church by four o'clock so they could go over the vows and instructions before the rehearsal.

The 'gang' will decorate after the rehearsal dinner. Jake isn't sure what the bridal party will come up with for decorations; Jess said he'd spearhead the decorating. Oh boy, Jake thought to himself, *this may be a trip*.

The ladies dressing room is down stairs, and very nice. It has a really spacious bathroom with double sinks and lots of full-length mirrors. In the lounge room, there are three love seats, three wing chairs and several folding chairs lined up against the wall. The colors in the dressing room are centered on mauve and mint, which will be perfect for pre-wedding pictures.

The men's bathroom is nice too, with one full-length mirror. There are also mirrors above the two sinks. The lounge room has a love seat and two wing chairs, along with a bench. Folding chairs also line one wall.

All clothes will be brought to the church the evening before the wedding to save confusion in the morning. Angela was delighted with this suggestion from Mam.

Emily will be coordinating the reception, and she, Mia and Beth will take care of making coffee, punch, regular and raspberry ice tea. They will also put all the paper products and utensils in place and set up a *Gift Table* and show the men where and how to place the head table. The men will also set up a second Gift Table in the back of the Sanctuary for guests to place their gifts. The ushers will inconspicuously move the gifts downstairs.

Emily loves to entertain, and now Beth will be learning how to be a hostess and organize functions.

Barstow will be the muscle (and he has plenty of it) when they need it, as well as stock communion and other supplies for the ceremony. His boisterous laugh could be heard at times when he was arranging things, especially the unity candle stand – he just couldn't decide how to situate it on the podium.

Jani, Pam and Carrie had already put their heads together. During the reception, they were planning on decorating the turquoise tank with bows, streamers and anything else they could find. Jani will be going to the City to pick up the balance of the things they had ordered at the Bridal Boutique and would pick up the decorating supplies at that time. The ladies have to be sure Jake doesn't find out what they were planning or he might hide the little vehicle.

They also have to get the Unity Candles they had forgotten on their last trip. Carrie will go with Jani since they still have to pick out a dress for her.

Jani knows the bride and groom are planning on riding the turquoise tank back to their apartment to change clothes after the wedding; before they take off on the Gold Wing. She had heard Jake talking to Dad about it. He will hook up the sidecar for the trip to hold suitcases: but she hadn't heard where they would be going, and Dad sure wouldn't spill the beans.

John and Josie would be bringing the gifts home in the Jimmy; and put them in the apartment for the newlyweds to put away later. Mam knows they will want to reexamine all of the gifts because they will not be able to remember where a lot of them came from. She'll just set them on the new carpet in their living room.

Angela and Kelli will be making the netted bird seed throw balls. They will not use rice because the birds eat it, get a drink of water, and the rice swells up in their craws and they die. They are putting a small white plastic dove on each 'ball' for a souvenir.

Almost everything was ready for this very special couple to become one flesh in Christ.

Wednesday about two o'clock, the County Inspector had gotten to Annabelle's land; and both the septic and well had been approved. The inspector gave Sonny the written approvals. As soon as the man left Sonny took off running to Wiley's shop. When he ran past the amphitheater, he made a mental note that Pam was on the steps journalizing again.

Sonny handed Wiley the Permits: and he and Wiley started rejoicing together. Wiley called Barstow and Jake to let them know the exciting news. Now they could do the finishing work, and Annabelle's new home could be delivered before too long. Wiley would call *United Homes* right away and set up a delivery date.

Wiley wouldn't tell the family until the home was set on the foundation, which couldn't be finished until the home was in its exact spot. However, the stem wall footings were in place.

He would put together a nice dinner for them for a surprise

when he brings them home, and was already imagining their surprised looks. It wouldn't be much of a chore to move them – they didn't have anything.

As Sonny started to leave the blacksmith shop, Wiley stopped him by saying, "Do you have your driver's license?"

"Well, yes I do, why?" Sonny answered with his own question, as he pulled the wallet out of his back pocket and handed the license to Wiley. Wiley looked at the license then handed it back to Sonny.

"I've been thinking, since you are going to be doing a lot of running around for Jake and me, you may need some temporary wheels. I've got this old black Chevy truck. It's fully insured and needs to be driven: so how would you like to drive it for a spell?" Wiley inquired.

"Wow, do you mean it?" Sonny exclaimed.

"Sure do, Sonny," Wiley assured him, "I see you trotting everywhere, having wheels will make your work go faster. So here are the keys. The Registration and Insurance Card are in the glove box."

Wiley paused as he pointed to an extra key on the ring before he went on; "This extra key here is to my shop, so if you need anything you can get in when I'm not here."

Sonny was blown away that Wiley would trust him so much, "Wow, Mr. Wiley, I swear I will take care of your truck and will not abuse the entry key to this shop."

On his way home Sonny had to pass the amphitheater again. He wanted to stop and show Pam the truck, but he really felt he shouldn't intrude in her world right now.

MYSTERY MOUNTAIN THREE

Jake Visits Roscoe & Ira Visits Lenore

"Greetings Roscoe," Jake said to his old friend as he walked into his office, "I'm here today to see Roscoe Martin, the Mayor."

"You don't need a reason to come to my office, Jake Judd, you're always welcome," Roscoe responded, "but what do you need Mayor Martin for?"

Jake told him about putting the basketball teams together, and that they might end up having to get the portable hoops, and if they do can they get permission to hold the games in the *Town Square*. Roscoe didn't see any problem at all, and felt like this was really a worthy cause. He also thought a nice ballpark might be in order, with bleachers, a clubhouse and dugouts next to *DoSoPa*. There is certainly plenty of room right there and we have more than enough money in the *Town Building Fund* that would cover the cost of materials if they could round up workers.

"When we don't have to pay for the labor, we really come out on top of a project," Mayor Roscoe informed Jake, "you, Wiley and Barstow think about it."

"Now I want to talk to Grandpa Martin." Jake continued.

"Oh," Roscoe's voice turned to concerned, "has Beth goofed up?"

"No," Jake assured him, "but I get the feeling that something is really troubling her; something major. Do you have any idea what it is? Beth has come so far and I hate to see anything haunting her."

"Jess and I have been trying to figure out that very thing,

Jake," Roscoe began, "I know it's something from her past - that she can't get past. She's pulled this 'zone out' on both of us. Jess is pretty concerned about her too. Your little brother hasn't made any improper advances toward her. In fact, his spirit is checked if he even looks at her too long of a time. He can feel her withdraw if she thinks he might be getting too close. Jess is sure becoming a fine young man, Jake. He and I talk about Beth's situation, but we just don't have any answers. I know she's excited about starting the *petting zoo,* but once in a while she'll even *'zone out'* while talking about it - and that's what makes me believe it is something serious. We've both tried to get her to open up, but she won't."

Jake could really feel the remorse his friend was harboring while talking about his granddaughter.

"I'm sure I've contributed to the problem by not keeping better tabs on her while she was growing up. Perhaps if I would have made time for her, like I didn't, whatever is eating her wouldn't have happened." Beth's grandpa went on.

"My dear friend," Jake came back firmly, "you have no blame in her past. You tried to keep in contact with her. It's not your fault her father died, there wasn't any way you could have prevented Junior's car accident. You certainly couldn't have prevented Pat from marrying Alan Becker. It would not have been right for you to try to take Beth away from Pat, besides you didn't know how this Alan was forcing Beth to live. Something tells me that when you wrote her, she never got the letters, they were intercepted. Have you asked her if she received any of your letters?"

"I slightly mentioned the letters a couple of times, but never asked her directly. Maybe I should ask her out right?" Roscoe suggested.

"I think that might be a good place to start." Jake urged him.

"Man, I sure miss Alice; she would have been able to talk to our granddaughter. I'm still lost without Alice even after eighteen years; she never even got to see Beth. Pat was pregnant with her when Alice passed away. Sometimes I get so depressed that I wish I could die and go to meet her," Roscoe said sadly, "but then who would be left to watch after Beth? I know she is in good hands at the ranch, but I'm still responsible for her, she is my family. Perhaps when she gets married I will be able to lay this burden down, but I can't now."

The two men sat in silence for quite a while, and then Jake gave his old friend a good-bye hug, reminding him that the wedding was the fifteenth. Sometimes when someone is hurting – just a silent presence can ease some of the pain. Just to know someone cares.

Ira decided to make a trip to see Lenore Patton. As he stepped in her front office, it was almost as if she was waiting for him.

"Greetings Ira," she said almost snappy, "it's about time you came to see me!"

Shocked, Ira answered with a question, "How'd you know I was coming?"

"Oh, I've been expecting you since I heard how you love math, and how good at it you are. You sure took your sweet time coming to see me," she answered him, still somewhat snappy, "not many people love figures like we do."

Still surprised, Ira continued, "How do you know how I did in school? I didn't go half the time."

"I know that too," Lenore insisted, "but I still kept tabs on you. Don't forget your math teacher, Naomi Wescott, and I have been best friends since our grade school years."

"Aaah, yes," Ira said thoughtfully, "Miss Wescott. I do remember her; I always felt like she didn't like me."

"Quite the opposite, Ira," Lenore continued, "she knew what you were capable of, and your laxity attitude irritated her. She felt you were wasting your good mind."

"You're joshing me," Ira projected, "Miss Wescott thought I had a good mind?"

"She sure did," Lenore confirmed, "now, what brings you here?"

"I want to buy yer business," Ira blurted out bluntly, "but I don't have any money, so I guess I'll just leave."

Ira had given up already. The idea suddenly seemed farfetched and he was making a fool of himself.

"Not so fast, Ira Carson," Lenore insisted with an air of authority, "you just sit back down and listen."

Ira sat back down obediently as Lenore told him her story.

"True, I want to sell this business. A big BUTT is – not to an outsider. I've had three good offers for my business and I've turned them down. As you know I was a *Woods People* as I was growing up, and I loved math. Right out of school I met Lance Patton, and three years later we were married. You remind me so much of my late husband Ira, he was tall and scraggly, with the animal hanging on his chin too.

"He was a good worker – and – saver, and he loved the people here in *Raincroft*. The *Woods People* were having a problem getting to the City to get their taxes done, and were being really put down because of their illiteracy. Plus, they were being ripped off, and that really made Lance angry. He swore to put an end to HIS people being terrorized by unscrupulous accountants. He made me promise to keep his promise alive.

"So, Lance and I decided to open an accounting business; mainly to take care of our friends in the woods. My business has mushroomed, and many of my accounts are second generation families. I will not allow the *Woods People* to be abused by anyone for any amount of money. I will keep my promise to my husband.

"After only three years of marriage, Lance went down into the canyon to rescue a friend, and never came back up. I was six months pregnant with our first child. Our daughter, Marissa, was born three months after Lance disappeared. My husband, of course, never met his daughter. I know he will see her in Heaven, because he knew Jesus.

"Sure, we can be uncouth, but most of us *Woods People* are honest, we are truepennies. Most didn't know how to do their finances; not even write a check. Now, many of my friends have their checks come to my office, where I have opened a joint checking account for each of them and myself. I pay their bills and taxes and give them the cash that is left over. An outsider would have zero compassion on these people.

"Besides, an Accountant is a Fiduciary position, and I'm not about to sell my business to a blabber beak. You are not a motor mouth, Ira; I've been watching you for several years. I think you have probably gone through most of your wild oats years, and are ready to settle down. This is hard work, many long hours, and even some heartaches.

"I promised Lance when he set me up in business that I would never do anything to injure our families – the *Woods People*. I will keep that promise to him.

"So, Ira, here's my one and only proposal, I don't mess around with counteroffers. You will start studying immediately. I have a complete set of DVDs' on learning accounting. I do not have time to teach you – but Josie, your blood mother, will. She will teach you the computer at the same time. You now know the passcode to get into the mountain, so you get started with her right away to learn accounting. I'm glad you are already versed in lots of the terminology. I've talked to Josie and she says Little Joe has the Family Room computers finished. Besides, with Todd having a computer at home, you can study double-time."

"You and Josie have discussed me – and this?" Ira asked Lenore shaking his head in amazement.

"Many times," she told him, "now that you are one of her sons she has a special interest in you. I will be going over each file with you after you have been with Josie for three months. That should be adequate time for your basic training. Then you will come to work here. You will show up by eight o'clock in the morning, and work until the day's work is done. Some days you might only work until ten o'clock in the morning, but others until ten o'clock in the evening – until the work is finished.

"You will be earning forty percent of the net profits, and I will be keeping sixty percent of the nets. You will still be bringing home a lot more than you currently are from the Mark's Mill. After I'm sure you can handle the business and the people, I will leave for Albuquerque to live with my widowed daughter and two grandkids.

"After I leave for Albuquerque, you will continue to send me forty percent of the net income for the balance of the five years, and then your Contract with me will be Paid in Full. You will also covenant to keep the unorthodox books for my family and friends, and never sell to an outsider. With your permission I'll have Roscoe draw up the Agreement. Are you all right with this? Can I call this business sold?"

She held out her hand to shake.

As Ira took her hand to accept her proposal, he was so astounded he couldn't speak. So, he just nodded. He couldn't believe the break this fine woman was giving him, mostly to honor the memory of her late husband's wishes. The terms were just what he had been mulling over in his mind, and discussing with Jake.

"Here are the Accounting studies; I'll have the sale as of July first." Lenore told him as she handed him a case of DVDs, "now I've got to buy another desk for you."

"I can use that little student desk right there." Ira told her.

"No, you can't," she responded, "a little boy by the name of Wilson comes in to do his homework at that desk. I love to watch him as he is learning to use the calculator I put there for him. He sure is a cute little guy, twelve years old I understand. Been coming in about six or eight months now, even when there isn't any school in session. Loves to work with figures. He makes up problems, and then solves them. Please keep that desk for him."

"I sure will," Ira promised her, "I know the kid. He's the boy that Wiley wants to adopt."

"And marry his mom Annabelle." Lenore added.

(Being the town accountant means you know almost everything about everyone.)

Ira could hardly wait to write to Leslie with the exciting news. Leslie's praying for him crossed through the back of his mind – for only a fleeting moment.

"And by the way," Lenore added, "I own this building; it's in the deal."

Kid's Basketball Meeting

As Annabelle and the two boys waited for Wiley to pick them up for the trip to the amphitheater for the Basketball-Organizational Meeting, the boys were thinking pretty hard.

"Mom, did Wiley mean it when he said he'd take us even without you?" Wilson asked.

"He sure did Wilson, 'is biggest dream is ta hav' a fam'ly." Mom replied.

"Has Wiley told you he loves you?" Wayne asked him mom.

"No Wayne, he hasn'. He'll not take ar' 'lationship any deeper 'til he 'as both o' ya boy's blessin's." Annabelle assured the boys.

"Why does he think we are so important? He doesn't need our permission," Wayne continued, "you're grow ups."

"But ya two boys ar' a very importan' part o' me, an' Wiley says we come as a package." Mom explained to them.

A few minutes later Wayne continued, "But if you guys get together, that means you'll sleep together too, huh?"

"Yes, son," Annabelle responded to his point-blank question, "if Wiley an' I gets married we will sleep together. But not 'til we gets married."

"You never slept with my dad, why?" Another point-blank question from Wayne.

"Caus' yur dad was in too much pain an' couldn' be tuched." Annabelle replied.

Both of the boys took deep breaths, and gave out heavy sighs. Annabelle believed Wayne knew what he was asking in the deeper sense. Wilson just thought Wiley would be sleeping beside his mom.

"Do you love Wiley, Mom?" Wayne asked another point-blank question.

"I don' know, we've not been thinkin' that way yet. I know I really like bein' aroun' him, he makes me feel good an' he makes me laugh. He makes you boys laff too, an' thas' important to laff as a fam'ly. Been a lon' time since we laffed. I know what good care he 'could give us. I know he 'could keep us safe'." Annabelle told her boys.

"I think Wiley loves you – 'cause I see how he looks at you." Wayne remarked.

"I know he loves yu boys – for yurselves – just 'cause you ar' yu." She assured them.

As Wiley pulled in the driveway, the boys jumped in. They were anxious to be getting involved in a friendly competition game. The boys were strangely silent as they rode.

Annabelle smiled at Wiley as she told him, "They'r' jus' thinkin' hard."

Wiley squeezed her hand gently.

At the amphitheater eighteen boys had shown up and were sitting on the concrete steps. Deputy Homer started laying out the plans for the friendly ball games. He cautioned everyone that this was strictly for fun, and no bullies were allowed. If someone were being 'nasty' they would be sent packin'. As Homer talked excitement was increasing, and it was looking like Homer had hit a winner. Most of the boys had parents seated around the Square taking in everything.

"Now," the deputy continued, "it's time to select teams. Wiley, you stand right here and I'll, I'll - stand right here – right where I'm standin' now… Wiley will call the first player he wants, and then I'll call the first one I want. Then Sonny will call one for Wiley's team and Jake'll call one for my team. Wiley, who do you pick first?"

"I pick Wilson Close." Wiley shouted.

"I pick Ronnie Baker," Homer shouted.

"I pick Wayne Close for Wiley's team." Sonny shouted.

Seemed as though they thought shouting would put enthusiasm in the boys.

"I pick Max Monroe for the Deputy's team." Jake shouted.

One by one the boys were all assigned to teams. Each team ended up with nine players.

"Now, our first practice will be Tuesday afternoon about five o'clock. And the first game will be Saturday at ten o'clock." Homer informed everyone.

"Now, each team will choose an' vote on a name - for the other team an' what colors they will be. That's right, each team gets to name the other team an' choose the opposing teams colors. This was Sonny's idea to spur some fun. Be prepared Tuesday evening at practice to vote on all names submitted." Homer told everyone.

Grumbles came from all the boys, and they looked at each other like their decisions were close to the end of the world. Their opponents would probably give them terrible names and colors, so each figured they had better do some brown-nosing. Sonny got a few tight lips, but he just smiled.

Wiley walked over to the large galvanized tub beside a plastic basket, "Treats for everyone." The big man hollered at all the kids.

As the boys came running, some of their small siblings were coming in from the audience too. But Wiley had anticipated that and brought plenty.

Seven Souls for Christ

Todd Carson had sat right down by Kelli when he walked in church this morning. Since she usually sits in the third row, it has always been a bit too close to the Pastor for Todd's liking and he usually sat a couple of rows back from her. Kelli had taken a hold of his hand as he sat down, and smiled at him. It made him feel good.

Pastor John was preaching on salvation, what true confession and acceptance of Christ means. "When you truly accept the Lord Jesus Christ as your Savior and Lord, you must turn away from and rebuke the evil things of the world. You can no longer take the Lord's name in vain, He hears every time you call Him a dirty word, how do you think that makes Him feel? Your body is the temple of the Holy Spirit, and you must be considerate with what you do to His Temple. A small glass of wine won't kill your temple, but drinking too much will. You can no longer be a winebibber.

"What about smoking? Each cigarette you smoke kills part of the Temple of God, because it kills your brain cells; it forces your body to not yield to the Holy Spirit.

"The God Head is a tri-unity. It is a three-in-one. Not three separate beings, but three different beings in one. The Father, The Son and The Holy Ghost. When you receive one – you receive all three – they cannot be separated. As earthlings we can't completely understand the concept, but when we get to Heaven we will.

"Here's an example – You have an arm – it's connected to your body. Even if something happens and you lose that arm – it's still your arm – it will always be your arm no matter where it is. You just do not have the power to reattach it to your body. Christ does. He is like an arm of God, part of Him. He detached from God and came to earth to die on the cross for our sins, but He was and is still God, and went back to be reunited with God at the ascension.

"At the Rapture, Christ will reattach us to our complete bodies. We will be whole again, just like Christ is. Your bodies will come out of the grave to be reunited with your soul and spirit. Your soul and spirit never die, at the very moment of death your soul and spirit either go to Heaven or Hell. Your eternity is sealed at the moment you die.

"Listen right now to what the Holy Spirit might be saying to your spirit. Yes, the Holy Spirit talks to you by way of your spirit. You are body, soul, spirit, a tri-unity just like the God Head. You are made in Christ's image; He is your Creator and Father. You did not get here because an ameba spawned you. Eternal God created you in His likeness. You are His creation and His child, and He loves you very much. Genesis 1:26 – God used making mankind in the plural: ""'Let US make man in OUR image, after OUR likeness.'"" The Tri-Unity of the Godhead is in the very first chapter of the Bible.

"God is not willing that any should perish. But He gave us Free Wills, and it is our choice to either believe the absolutes of the Bible, and go to Heaven. Or, to not believe or water down the absolutes and go to Hell. Heaven and Hell are very real places and YOU choose where you will go.

"Jesus Christ was born of the Virgin Mary. The Holy Spirit fell on her and planted the fertilized seed in her by one of the greatest miracles of all time. The baby Jesus was both fully God and fully man. The God part didn't need to be birthed through the canal, but the man part did, and thus the virgin birth.

"Never let anyone tell you there is another way to salvation except for the acceptance of Jesus Christ, His dying on the cross, shedding His Blood, going to the grave, and rising again on the third day. The blood and pericardial fluid that flowed from his side on the cross when the soldier pierced his side is the cleansing stream for your sins.

"You have never done something so bad that the Blood of

Jesus Christ can't cover it. There is no sin that the Savior's Blood cannot cover. You can have forgiveness, every one of you. We are told Christ would die for our sins clear back in Isaiah 55.

"God has a *'sea of forgetfulness'* for our sins to be remembered no more. Please jot down these verses and read them later, *Micah 7:19, Jeremiah 31:34, Hebrews 8:12 and 10:17.* That means that if you are really sincere when you repent, your sins will never be remembered again. You will only be judged on those things you do for Christ when you get to the *Judgement Seat of Christ* that <u>all Christians</u> will have to stand before. *"Second Corinthians 5:10,* tells us all Christians will be judged by Christ.

Luke 16:19-31 tells us that non-Christians will stand before <u>The Great White Throne</u>. *You* make the decision where you will spend eternity. Your soul and spirit will never die, it lives forever. Paul tells us in *Second Corinthians 5:8 (KJV), "To be absent from the body is to be present with the Lord."* This is for the Christians who die <u>saved</u>.

"On the other end, *Psalms 8:17 (KJV),* warns all, *"The wicked shall be turned into Hell, and all the Nations that forget God."* They are both very real places. You cannot take God's words and make them a lie, or take a lie and make it God's Word. God never changes, neither does His Word. John 3:3 says you must be Born Again to see the Kingdom of God. There is *no* other way.

"After you repent and give your life to Jesus Christ, the absolute only way to have salvation, you need to be baptized. Baptism is not a pre-requisite to save your soul, only Christ can do that, but baptism accompanies salvation to help attain perfection and to publicly announce you are now a *Child of God.*

"I know this has been a pretty serious sermon today, but eternal life is serious. Please, everyone, bow your heads and close your eyes, no one looking around. Has this message touched your soul? Do you know if you were to die today where you will be spending eternity? The moment you die you either go to Heaven or Hell. There is no in-between. Death is final.

"Who in this audience wants to repent and make peace with God today, and be sure the blood of Jesus washes you? If you do, please stand up and walk to the front and kneel before the Lord, so Elder Barstow or I can pray with you. Seal your eternity right now as Emily plays *'Just as I am, without one plea, because Thy Blood was shed for me, and as Thou bid's me, I come to You Lord Jesus, I come.'* Will you come right now?"

As Pastor John and Elder Barstow stood silently on the steps to the platform Todd Carson stood up. He was weeping as he started toward the front of the church. A tearful Kelli stood up and took his hand to walk forward with him. As he knelt on the step and rested his elbows on the prayer bench, Pastor John came down to pray with him and right there in front of the whole church Todd Carson asked for forgiveness of his sins, and made a commitment to the Lord Jesus Christ and Him crucified.

Annabelle Close also stood up weeping, and started toward the front. Wiley caught up and took her hand to walk with her to meet Jesus. Elder Barstow came down to pray with her as she asked for forgiveness of her sins and made a commitment to Christ. To her surprise, she felt a smaller hand go inside of hers, and as she looked - her oldest son, Wayne, was weeping also and saying the sinner's prayer to receive the only way of Salvation, our Lord Jesus Christ.

As Todd and Kelli were holding each other and weeping together, Annabelle, Wayne and Wiley were holding each other and weeping together also.

There was a new couple to *Raincroft* that no one seemed to know much about at the alter weeping as Pastor John was praying with them.

Barstow was now holding and praying with an older man, and Mia was cradling a young girl.

Several minutes passed as souls were being cleansed and healed.

Finally, Pastor Stoddard stood back up as he said, *"Luke 15:10 tells us the angels in Heaven are rejoicing with our Lord for these seven forgiven souls, knowing they will be coming to get them when the time comes for them to meet The Lord.* That's right, the angels come and take Christians to Heaven at the moment of death. Read Luke chapter sixteen.

"The Baptismal service will be next Sunday evening; I hope you can all join us in rejoicing.

"Now, if everyone will stand for the Benediction. *"May The Lord bless you and keep you, and make His face shine down on you. May He make His grace abound around you, and keep you safe and at peace, until we meet again. Amen."*

Jake had been watching Sonny during the service, and could see how obviously moved the young man was. Homer had joined Sonny for the service, and Jake knew the deputy to already be a Christian, and was probably praying for the young man beside him during the service. Ira and Billy had even slipped into the back row, and were listening. Seems like the Holy Spirit always gives Pastor John the message needed for the exact time.

He thought he saw Billy Carson wiping his eyes as Jake was scanning the audience – apparently watching for anything wrong?? His eyes kept returning to the new couple in *Raincroft*, and then to scanning the audience again.

Sonny's eyes were watching Jake watch.

A Shopping Trip & A Cast Removed

With a most grateful heart Wiley loaded his family into the Jeep to head back to Annabelle's. He asked the boys if they were hungry, and they both wanted pizza again, so they stopped at *Lil' Italy's* to eat.

Wiley said they needed to go to the City in the morning to get some nice clothes to wear to the wedding. He wants *'the family'* to look the best possible. Wiley would pick everyone up about nine o'clock. He could see the boys exchanging glances in the rear-view mirror, and they were obviously both excited about a trip to town. It probably meant they could go to *The Sweet Dragon*.

Wiley smiled thinking to himself, Bribery? No, just a family function. Wiley's heart was so full of thanksgiving he could hardly speak. Two of his family had met Jesus, and he knew Wilson would eventually also.

The joyous big man wanted to give Annabelle a big hug and a kiss when he arrived the next morning, but he had to keep things cool to not offend the boys. He could at least squeeze her hand while they were riding – and be able to look at her beautiful countenance.

He had snapped in the plastic windows on the jeep. It was starting to rain again. Annabelle was secure knowing if the lightning and thunder started again, she and the boys would be safe. Death possibilities were very real in her mind, but now she knows that if she or Wayne were to die, they would both go to Heaven. She also knew Wilson would come around. Especially since this wonderful man sitting beside her will keep talking to him.

"When I prayed this morning, I asked the Lord to clear things up so we could stay dry today as we shop." Wiley said to the family.

He could see both boys' expressions about God stopping the rain just because Wiley prayed. But to their amazement, by the time they were about half way down the hill, the sun was shining. He stopped the Jeep and the boys learned how to take out the plastic windows.

Wiley puckered his lips up at Annabelle, and she puckered hers back at him. Her twinkling eyes knew he meant "kiss, kiss."

As they pulled into the City, Wiley asked the boys, "Do you want to shop or eat first? And, where do you want to eat?"

"Eat at *The Sweet Dragon* first." Came the dual answers from the back seat.

The big man was sure what their answer would be and had already turned down the street to the eatery.

Wiley said grace, and while they were eating, Wiley asked Wayne, "I understand you really enjoyed looking at the four foundations for the low-income rentals?"

"I sure did." Came the response from Wayne.

"I saw them too, but didn't walk all over them like Wayne did," Wilson chimed in, "he followed Sonny all over measuring everything."

"What was your opinion of the project, Wayne?" The big man asked grinning.

"Well, Sonny and I talked about the bolts being good, and even a half spiral stairway to upstairs so it wouldn't take up so much room. Sonny said each unit would be about 575 feet minus the walls using two by sixes. We also like how the plumbing is all in one spot in the middle of each side that'll save money on extra pipes. We also think big picture windows that really open would be good so people can move their big stuff in through them." Wayne was getting so far into the question that he was saying 'we'.

"Wow, I'm impressed. You picked up on everything. Good job Wayne, hurray for you," Wiley was grinning from ear to ear as he high-fived his eldest son, "did Jake show you anything else?"

"Yea," Wayne answered, "but it wasn't as fun as the big projects." Wiley caught Annabelle's eyes, she was grinning from ear to ear too.

"Gonna cost a lot of money to finish it." Wilson cut in.

Pretty good, Wiley was pondering to himself, *a Contractor and an Accountant. That'll work. God really knows how to answer prayer! Wayne will probably be better at basketball, since it can be rough, but Wilson will be able to keep tabs on the scoring. Perfect. I need to know where their talents point so I won't push them into anything they are not emotionally equipped to do.*

Annabelle was sitting across from him in the booth and kept accidentally – on purpose – leaning her knee against Wiley's. It was actually bothering his concentration; but he wanted to sit there forever. Wilson said he wanted to get Wiley's money's worth, and kept eating until they thought he would bust.

It was an upscale department store Wiley took them to for their new clothes.

"I think your mother should model for us, don't you guys?" He asked the boys.

"Yea, model for us, Mama, we'll pick out some clothes for you to try on." They both squealed - and with that they were gone to the racks.

"Great," Annabelle remarked, "what kin' o' a floozy will they be dressin' me up as."

"We'll see." Wiley grinned at her.

Annabelle started looking through some rack on her own, and then pulled back as she told Wiley, "Everythin' here is so 'spensive."

"It's all right, my little belle, I want you to look magnificent. You pick out anything you want." He encouraged her.

The boys came back with two outfits each.

"Try mine on first." Wilson told his mom.

"No, try mine on first." Wayne echoed.

"Tell ya what, boys, I'll mix 'em up so I don' know who's' is who's'." She told them as she took off into the dressing room.

A few moments later she came out with a short dress that was about two sizes too small. She really looked funny, but she was determined to go with the flow, so she strutted around for the guys – who were cracking up. Wiley would have been rolling on the floor if he knew he wouldn't be arrested.

"Try another one." Wayne told her, so she headed back to the dressing room.

This time the dress was about four sizes too big for her and it was dragging the floor. The neckline went clear down to her waist as she was holding her front together. Again, the three fellas were cracking up. The shoulders were so big that she couldn't keep both of them up at the same time. She couldn't let go of the front, and when she let go of one shoulder the other one would slide down to her elbows. She had never seen her boys' laugh like that, deep rolling cackles that were so infectious she was laughing too.

The next one had no mid-section, was again two sizes too small and almost showed her underpants. She hesitated about going out, but decided she would be good for another laugh, so she took a big breath and stepped out of the dressing room to the hilarious squeaks from all three guys. She didn't stay out in that one very long, she high tailed back into the dressing room before any other customers would see her.

The last one was a big one too. The gathered bodice, which was supposed to go to the waist, was down around her hips, and the bottom was all uneven and dragging the floor.

"Loo's like one of ya thin's I'm fat an' the other one thin's I'm a teeny bopper." She told her now crying audience, who were unable to speak.

By the time she came back out in her own slacks, the fellas had settled down.

"This time I get to pick out a couple of outfits." Wiley told everyone as he started looking through the racks.

He had gone to the suit racks instead of the dress racks. Annabelle was right behind him. Then the entourage moved to the fancy dress racks.

"Good legs." He whispered in her ear. She nudged him softly with her elbow.

Wiley picked out two suits and one long gown. She tried on the yellow suit first. The guys loved it and instead of laughs, she was getting wolf whistles and affirmations. The second suit was a pale blue with soft magenta flowers and mint leaves. The fellas really liked that suit on her. It had a fake back belt on the jacket and two front pockets at the waist. The skirt was mid-calf with a slit up the back.

"Is that torn?" Wilson asked.

"No, it's for her legs to move," Wayne responded, "otherwise she couldn't walk."

"Wiley could carry her like Ira did Leslie." Wilson came back.

"I don't think so." Wayne told his brother.

Annabelle grinned at Wiley, who grinned back. The boys seem to notice everything, and it looks like Wilson thinks Wiley can do anything.

It was a royal blue gown that reached to her ankles. There were sequins all up and down one side in the form of big feathers. The sleeves went to the elbows, with 'drag through the gravy' lace at the edges. The cowl neckline would be perfect for white pearls. Annabelle looked like a movie star in the gown, it was absolutely astounding.

There goes Wiley's heart – Pitter-Pat, Pitter-Pat.

Even the sales clerk came over to remark how lovely she looked in the gown. "We'll take the gown and the pale blue two-piece suit." Wiley announced.

"Both?" Wilson asked, "But that's a lot of money."

Wiley snickered as he roughed Wilson's hair.

Now to the suit department. The salesman came out and took the measurements of the three men. The boys didn't seem to be having as much fun looking at the racks of suits. They weren't funny like the dresses. They found three matching men's suits.

"Now you and your boys will be triplets." The salesman told Wiley – who just smiled very pleasantly.

They found royal blue silk shirts for all three. Wayne was rubbing them like he was touching something breakable. He seemed to really like nice things. Wilson was more interested in the characters on the ties. They found white ties with deep blue scrolling all over them and even white hankies with the same deep blue trim.

"Whatta we need these for?" Wilson asked.

"In case we cry at the wedding." Wayne answered him.

After they had gotten belts, shoes and socks for the guys, they had to return to the ladies' shoe department so Mom could try on shoes to match her gown and suit.

"Looks like the whole store is coordinated." Wayne quipped as his mother found some royal blue satin shoes to match her gown.

They had a lower heel so they would be more comfortable for a longer period of time.

Wiley ushered the family over to the jewelry department where he picked out a three-stranded necklace and earrings set made from tiny pearls. It was very feminine.

"Like you." He whispered in her ear.

Next, to the Cosmetic Department. Here the boys could have some fun smelling colognes. Wiley bought Annabelle a bottle of Estee Lauder Beautiful. The Beautiful had a gilded gold gift pack with it. The gold case was filled with all kinds of makeup and lotions. She had never had such a thing, and was looking at and smelling everything in it.

The boys had been spraying the little sniff cards with different colognes to see which one they liked the best.

"Here's the one we like the best for you." Wayne told the big man.

"But you are picking out some for each of you." Wiley told them.

"We are?" Wilson asked.

"That's right, pick out the one you want to wear." Their benefactor instructed them.

More sniffing.

Annabelle was still looking and smelling the items in her

gold gift pack as the boys were trying to decide what they wanted. Finally, they had apparently agreed on the same fragrance for both of them, it's called Paco. They thought the name was funny, Paco.

Wiley bought himself a bottle of Paco to match the boys as he told them, "We don't want to clash with our stinky."

A slip and panty hose pretty much finished their shopping, and that didn't take long. By the time they got back to the jeep you could smell the two boys a mile away. Wiley cautioned them about using too much, that it would make them offensive to others. Reluctantly they agreed.

Wiley wanted to stop by the Christian Book Store. He wanted to purchase about a dozen nice Bibles. One for each one of his family, one for Todd and Sonny, and even one for Billy Carson. Apparently, he too had noticed Billy in the back row.

There was also a young lady that had popped into the back door of the church for several moments; she had a black brimmed hat on and a veil covering her face. He would have Barstow watch for her and slip her one of the Bibles.

Seems like nothing happens in *Raincroft* that either Jake or Wiley doesn't see.

On their way back to the Jeep Wayne and Wilson were popping between cars and peeking up at each other like ground squirrels. Three rough looking boys about fifteen or sixteen years old spotted them and started walking toward Wiley's boys with malice in their expressions.

When the two boys saw the troublemakers they both ran to get behind Wiley.

As the three boys approached they asked Wiley, "What do you think you are going to do? You're only one and there's three of us."

The big man smiled at them, and as he spoke to them with his booming voice they stepped back.

Wiley's voice was in itself threatening as he said to them, "Don't touch my boys or I'll get mad, and you don't want me mad. I'm only one, but one of me is more than you three together, and I really don't want to hurt you. I'm sorry you have bad home lives, and that you don't know Jesus Christ. I've just bought some Bibles at the book store, so instead of you fighting, read one of these." Wiley handed a Bible to each one.

The three boys took the Bibles as Wiley put his arm around each one of his boys and nodded at Annabelle to head to the Jeep.

The boys were still standing there watching Wiley as he drove off and nodded to them as he said, "A gentle word turns away wrath. Dear Lord, please take the three seeds I have planted and cultivate them."

"The Bibles are seeds?" Wilson asked.

"Yes son," Wiley answered, "we are to plant seeds where ever we go, and God will grow them."

"Is *"A gentle word turns away wrath"* in the Bible?"" Wayne asked.

"Yes son, you each get one of the Bibles we just purchased, pick your color, find *Proverbs 15:1* and read it for yourselves. Being meek does not mean you are weak. I didn't want to get physical with the boys and hurt them; that's meekness and compassion. But if they would have forced my hand I would have been stronger than the three together, and would have held them for the police." Wiley told the boys as they were feverishly looking through their new Bibles.

"Yea, I remember Jake and the Carson boys taking all six of us boys to the sheriff's office…" Wayne remarked.

As they started up the mountain, it was obvious that the boy's eyelids had gotten very heavy, and it didn't take too long until they were both asleep. Wiley pulled over and draped a blanket over the boys to keep them from chilling.

Annabelle was smiling like a princess at Wiley as she reached over and took his hand. She could never remember having this kind of fun before. She was really enjoying his company, and had never felt this warmness before. She poked out her lips in an air kiss, and Wiley returned one.

"The boys were askin' hard questions 'bout us while we were waitin' for ya, Wiley." She told him.

"That's great, sweetie, that means they are thinking." He remarked as he kept gently squeezing her hand back while they exchanged glances. He raised her hand up and kissed it gently. He just couldn't keep his eyes off her beautiful face.

Lord, he was thinking to himself, *I would have taken an ugly wife, but You are giving me this beautiful one. Thank you, Lord, for my family; I will be faithful to them. However, I sure would appreciate a few minutes alone with Annabelle. Just a few moments, Lord.*

Everyone was hanging their new clothes up so they wouldn't be wrinkled for Jake and Angela's wedding. The boys could hear some neighbors laughing and talking, and took off to tell them about their shopping trip.

"They sure won't be able to sneak up on their friends smelling like perfumed skunks." Wiley chuckled.

Wiley and Annabelle were alone; thank you Lord. They weren't sure for how long, so she was the first to become aggressive. She put her arms around him and tilted her head up to be kissed.

Wiley obliged her – and again – and again, so softly and tenderly. Words were unnecessary; they just loved holding each other.

"Annabelle," Wiley finally said, "You make me feel so funny and giddy. I know you were a very faithful wife to Wayne – but did you love him? I probably shouldn't ask, but Barstow said you probably didn't. Is Barstow right, Annabelle, like me, have you never been in love? Are all these feelings new to you too?"

She waited a bit before she answered, "I've nev'r been in love. I didn' get a chance to love Wayne; he was always so sick – even from the very beginnin'. It hurt if anyone touched him. He even slep' on his own cot so we wouldn't accidently touch in the night. It's amazing I 'ave two boys 'cause we were never lovers much. Barstow is right, thes' giddy feelin's are new ta me too, Wiley. But I like 'hem, I really like 'hem. How 'bout yu'?"

"Yes, Annabelle, I like them, I really like them too." He guaranteed the little wife he is claiming.

Jake had to make a trip to the City in the Jimmy the next morning to pick up the tuxedos, and finally get the cast off his arm.

When the doctor sawed the cast off, his skin was all flaky and white. Jake straightened the arm slowly, and kept moving it in and out. It was sore and stiff, and he would have to exercise it quite a bit to get it in shape for his wedding.

The doctor told him it looks good and gave him some cream to put on the scars and the flaking. Jake knew he would have long sleeves and a jacket on for the wedding, so he didn't think a white arm would be a problem. He just wanted to be sure he could lift his new wife with it. He wanted to carry her over the threshold of their home after the wedding the correct way, not like holding a bag of flour with one arm. And be able to drive the bike safely with his precious cargo sitting with him.

MYSTERY MOUNTAIN THREE

First Basketball Practice & Cell Phones

All eighteen boys showed up, along with the five men, for the first basketball practice at five Tuesday evening. Since they didn't have the portable hoops yet, they all headed for *DoSoPa* to play.

The baskets are mounted at exactly ten feet to the hoop ring for regulation height, but it is a bit difficult to bounce the balls on the dirt; however, this would have to work until a permanent plan could be hatched.

Jake was relaying to the men what Mayor Roscoe had told him about the *Town Building Fund,* and they need to put their heads together. Barstow told him that the Ranch could buy wholesale which should save them a bunch of money.

Wiley chimed in, "We can tell Todd what we are interested in and let him do some checking and see what he can come up with. Of course, the Town will compensate him for his work."

Playing was rough as was expected." The 'plays' were assigned to the players, and what the moves were called. After about an hour and a half of learning 'basketball lingo', Homer said he thought the boys' had enough for one evening, and it was time for treats. All the kids had kept an eye on the galvanized tub and plastic basket Wiley had brought, and were racing for them as Homer shouted,

"Dismissed, see everyone Saturday at ten o'clock sharp."

The rain had started again as Wiley pulled into Annabelle's driveway. The boys darted inside. Annabelle was waiting at the door. He could see her smiling lips – but right now he wouldn't be able to kiss them. He did give her a big hug – as the boys watched. He knew they were thinking about him touching their mother.

That's ok; he thought to himself, *they will see how folk greet each other when they care so much for each other.*

"Ira's going to buy Mrs. Patton's Accounting Business." Wilson stated right out of thin air trying to make conversation, and perhaps steer Wiley away from his mom.

"How do you know that?" Wayne asked his brother.

"I jus' know." Wilson assured him.

The lightning and thunder had started again.

"You don't have to leave yet, do you Wiley?" Annabelle asked him with a bit of anxiety in her voice.

"Yea, Mom's so afraid of the storm 'cause it makes our house shake." Wilson asserted.

"Sure, I'll hang around for a while." Wiley told the family.

Both boys sighed deeply as they started for their TV to see if they could pick up anything.

"The boy's ar' scared too." Annabelle told Wiley.

"I know, Sweetie, but when you get into your new home it will feel a lot safer to you all because it is a regular home." Wiley comforted her.

Annabelle poured him some raspberry ice tea as they sat down on the sofa to talk. Their talks were getting deeper and deeper into their pasts, and their likes and dislikes. Wiley really wanted to know all about his family, how the boys do in school, what she does all day while they are gone and about her childhood.

It was almost two hours later that the stormy racket was letting up. The trailer definitely swayed and shook in the wind. There were still a couple of holes in the roof that required attention, and he told Annabelle he would be out in the morning to fix them. As the water filled the buckets, the metal sound of the drips the noise changed from a metal sound to a water drip sound that was less noisy.

Sometimes when the thunder would crack Annabelle would jump into Wiley's arms for a moment of safety. Once Wilson came running from the bedroom and sat down close to Wiley. He was frightened too, and he somehow knew that this big man could protect him. Wiley put his arm around his boy.

He was mentally noting where more leaks were clanging down into the buckets. He sure wished at least one Casa was ready for occupancy; he would certainly put his family in a unit until their real home was finished.

Next morning, Wiley swung by the Canyon Casas. Sonny had two of the boys from jail working with him – Wayne and Ronnie Baker, unloading the semi that had arrived, and to his surprise Wilson was with them counting everything. He had gone 'to jail' with his brother again this morning. Wiley was so proud of both boys.

The fork lift was elevating the lumber on the building three foundation where Sonny had put blocks around the edge high enough so the lumber wouldn't sit in water. He was also watching carefully so the fork lift did not drive on to the green concrete to crack it.

Wayne seemed to be 'biting at the bit' to drive the fork lift… but that wasn't going to happen…even if he was Wiley Ronsons son.

Sonny was counting every piece against the packing slip, and checking the quality of each piece. Wilson was rechecking when Sonny handed him the packing list (with a big grin) after he finished it.

"We won't cut the steel bands around the lumber until we are ready to use them," Sonny was telling the fellas, "that way they won't warp out of shape so fast."

"Awesome job, Sonny," Wiley Atta Boyed him, "looks as though you've got everything under control. Guess I'll head on over to the lot to be sure everything is ready for Annabelle's new home to be brought in."

"It is," Sonny assured him, "when I went by this morning everything was well."

That's pretty hard work for Wayne, Wiley was thinking to himself as he headed to Annabelle's, *and little Wilson, counting everything. That's my boy.*

Annabelle was waiting for a big hug and kiss when Wiley pulled in. She was alone, and was going to make the most of it. As Wiley stepped inside the front door she didn't wait for him to take hold of her – she took hold of him. He tried to tell her what the boys were doing, but she had smooching on her mind – so he obliged her.

As they kissed over and over, he knew he must have this woman for his wife, he couldn't tell her yet without the boy's acceptance, but he really loves her from deep within him, and through her warm sweet kisses he could tell she really loves him too. Wiley could tell her affection is one of love, not of gratitude, and he was thanking his Lord. He held his woman close for over a half an hour before he knew he had to get on the roof and do more of the needed repairs before it started raining again.

After going back to his shop to check for messages and jobs, Wiley headed out to the Ranch. He wanted to see how much of the little barn foundation the three boys from jail had dug. Max Monroe, Chad Wall and Jimmy Price were working as he pulled in. The ground was soft from the rain over night, and the boys were just about finished. Barstow was overseeing the work as Wiley walked up to him. The boys had mud caked about two inches out the sides of their boots.

"Looking good." Wiley remarked.

"Yep, the boys are doing a good job. If the rain will let up a bit we can order the concrete as soon as we get the re-bar tied together in the ground." Barstow affirmed.

"Annabelle's place is ready for the home to be delivered," Wiley was telling Barstow, "but *United Homes* said they can't deliver the home until June 29th, so we're just going to have to wait. The home is so big that it's going to take both of their large tractors to bring it up the mountain. The family can live there without the stem-wall being completed for a couple of weeks; it will still be safer than what they are living in now."

Barstow certainly agreed.

"Now," Wiley continued, "I feel very sure that Annabelle

loves me – just for me, Barstow, I can tell it by the way she kisses me and looks at me. Man, I'm really head over heels for this woman. I'm still waiting for the boy's blessings however. I'm going to go over and see Tom Crane about getting a cell phone for her; I get worried about her being alone and not being able to call me in the event of trouble."

"Sounds like things are coming along for you, my friend," Barstow observed, "I'm glad you are comfortable that she really loves you now. A cell phone is a good idea; she is pretty isolated out there."

Tom was sitting in the Verizon office with his feet up on his desk as Wiley walked in.

"Looks like you need something to do," Wiley commented, "I want a cell phone for my future wife, nothing fancy on it, just some good service."

"You mean Annabelle?" Tom mentioned.

"News certainly does travel, doesn't it?" Wiley snickered.

Wiley picked out a powder blue telephone, and paid for the service policy. He could hardly wait to give it to her after he charged it and programmed his number into it, along with Dr. Lowery's, the Ranch, Jake's and a few others, including Sheriff Leo's. He wanted his boys with him when they surprise their mother. More bonding with my boys, he thought to himself.

The big man also wanted service for Sonny Boatright since he was going to be his Construction Foreman, and they needed a way to stay in contact with each other. He figured Sonny would like the royal blue one, with all the perks. This would certainly be a surprise to Sonny.

As soon as he got back to the shop he plugged both phones in to charge them. He knew Sonny was still on incarceration, but it doesn't seem like it, the kid loves to work now, and seems to enjoy doing anything. So much different than the roughneck that had gotten arrested.

When Wiley stopped by the Sheriff's office to give the sheriff and Homer Annabelle's and Sonny's new telephone numbers, both of his boys were already in the cell. Wiley chuckled as they ran out to greet him when he walked in.

"Got something for your mother, boys," he said to them, "and you'll be able to use it too."

He pulled the pretty blue cell out of his pocket. The boy's eyes got as big as dollars as Wiley was showing them how to use it.

"We've never had a telephone anywhere – ever," Wayne was saying, "what's our number? Can I call someone?"

Wiley showed them how to look at the contact list and then push the little green receiver button to call that person.

"Who can I call?" Wilson asked.

"Call me." Wiley answered.

Wilson started scrolling through the names, and then when Wiley's popped up he pushed the little green receiver button. Wiley's phone started ringing amid the boys' giggling, and he handed it to Wayne to answer.

Then Wayne wanted to make a call, so Wiley handed the phone to him. Wiley had programmed Annabelle's name on the Contact List so they would always know their number. He handed the boys a permanent marker to write their number on their forearms until they could memorize it.

After Wiley gave the sheriff Annabelle's and Sonny's new numbers, he asked Homer if he could take his boys with him to give their mother the surprise. Homer readily agreed. Wiley kept realizing that Homer was talking better and better. Plus, he couldn't help but notice how much the young man was filling out; he wasn't the scrawny deputy anymore.

The three guys pulled into their driveway. The boys jumped out and beat Wiley to the door announcing Wiley had a surprise for her.

"For me?" She asked, as Wiley stepped into the house.

Wilson started digging in Wiley's pocket for the little box; too excited to wait for a slow Wiley to fetch it. As soon as he had a grip on it he pulled it out, opened it, and handed the little powder blue phone to his mother.

She looked at it a moment, then up at Wiley as she whispered, "I ain' nev'r had a phone."

The boys were both trying to show her how easy it is to use.

"Here, push this little bar until you see who you want to call, then just push the green button. See, here's your name on the phone, with our phone number so you won't forget it." Wayne was saying.

"Now, you call Wiley." Wilson suggested.

As Annabelle started scrolling for his name she saw all the names this wonderful man had programmed in for her convenience. When she got to Wiley's name she pushed the green button and his phone started ringing. She was elated and grabbed Wiley and gave him a big hug. Pulling back just a bit, he kind of thought she might try and kiss him in front of the boys, and that wouldn't be a good idea yet, especially the passionate kisses she had started giving him.

"Now you and the boys won't be so isolated, and can get help when you need it." He told his exuberant family.

Wiley hadn't even gotten out of the woods before Wayne called him; "Do I need to go back to jail today?"

"No son, not today." Wiley answered his excited caller.

Ira was talking with John Stoddard and Emily as Wiley pulled in to give them the two new phone numbers. Ira was obviously flying high as Wiley walked up to the trio.

The young mountain man decided to start back at the beginning so Wiley and Sonny could hear everything about his visit to Lenore.

Sonny had popped in to the Ranch to see how the zoo project was going. He felt he should really keep track of things now that he is getting a Casa out of his work, and needs to be sure everything is going smoothly as he gives his benefactors the work they so richly deserve. Sonny listened intently to Ira's story and he was overjoyed for his big mountain friend.

When Ira finished, everyone was rejoicing. "The Lord sure works in mysterious ways, huh, Ira?" Emily said out loud, "And of course, I'll get you Leslie's address."

"Good, I'm glad you're here, Sonny," Wiley said to the kid,

"I've got a cell for you too." He handed the royal blue box to Sonny as he continued, "With you being our Construction Manager, we need to be able to keep in contact, and so this should do the trick."

As the young man took the phone and started scrolling through it, he was so emotional he couldn't speak. John Stoddard and Ira both took out their cells and programmed both Sonny's and Annabelle's numbers into their phones. Even though the young man had never had a cell phone, it took him about thirty seconds to figure the whole thing out. John smiled at Wiley; both knowing the kid was brilliant.

Finally, when Sonny could speak, his cracking voice said, "I can't believe how wonderful you guys are. I just can't believe it. Me, a nobody, to have friends like you."

"Well, Sonny," John Stoddard cut in, "we all feel blessed that you are one of us. We needed some young muscle, and a good mind around here, so we're thinking the Lord gave you to us."

There John went with that Lord business again, but Sonny wasn't going to say anything negative to spoil the moment.

First Basketball Game, Ballpark Plans & An Old Printer

Wiley dialed Annabelle's number to let her know he was on the way to pick up the boys and her for the game.

As she answered he greeted her, "Hi Sweetie, I'm on my way."

He realized he could say sweet nothings to her on the cell phone that the boys couldn't hear, how fantastic.

That alone is worth the price of her phone. He reckoned to himself.

He'd just have to be sure Annabelle was the one that answered.

The three were waiting as he pulled in, and the boys came running out and jumped in the Jeep. Annabelle followed as she was making 'eyes' at the big man. Wiley was sure he caught Wayne picking up on her flirting, but right then it didn't matter. He was so glad to see her again.

All boys showed up for the first game. Homer asked the boys if they had come up with names and colors for the opposing teams yet, but everyone said no.

"Well, I need 'hem by Tuesday night practice," Homer told the boys, "so we can get the uniforms ordered an' names an' numbers put on 'hem."

The teams got lined up and five were chosen from each to start the first quarter, two Forwards, two Guards and one Center.

The ground was still muddy after the overnight rain, plus it was starting to rain again. Homer didn't want a bunch of sick kids, so he dismissed everyone and said the Tuesday night practice was still on. The deputy apologized for their very first game being rained out.

So far, the year had been one of the rainiest they had seen for years, and the thunder and lightning had been atrocious.

The kids scampered into the dry amphitheater for treats before they left…the treats sure were not rained out.

Homer asked for the men to meet him at the Sheriff's Office.

Since Annabelle and the boys were with Wiley, the boys went to the cell to sit, and Wiley pulled up a chair for Annabelle. She was having a hard time seeing her boys in a jail cell, even with the door open. The men could see her disdain, and Jake hollered at them to come on out and join the meeting.

Annabelle's relief was obvious.

Homer had made some notes for consideration for the new ballpark, and he gave each man a copy of what he had drawn.

"I figgered we'll need a full-size ball court in case ar' teams gets challenged by outsiders, an' they need to know how to play the big fields. An' the big fields ar' ninety-four feet long an' fifty feet wide. As you can see on the plans the circles go from four-feet to twenty-two feet from the basket. Whatta ya think?" Homer inquired.

Jake spoke first, "Homer, did you draw up these court plans?"

"Yes, Mr. Jake, I sure did." The deputy responded.

"They're great; all the circles are spaced where they need to be," Wiley chimed in, "where did you get all the measurements?"

"Studying on the computer." Homer replied.

"These are as good as any I've ever seen." Sonny added.

"I'm proud of you Deputy." Barstow echoed.

The young deputy wasn't used to accolades, and was blushing as he said softly, "Thank you all."

"We'll study your plans and have another meeting," Jake announced, "it's obvious that we can't play in the mud. We'll just have to make a ball park a priority. The kids are all psyched up now about playing, and we've got to do whatever it takes to keep them occupied."

Everyone agreed. Hopefully Tuesday night for practice the rain wouldn't be a problem.

Barstow said he would be going to the City Monday, and, if it's okay with everyone, he will get two of the portable hoops to use in the interim. He would be taking Sonny with him.

As they left the Sheriff's Office, Sonny saw Pam in the back of the amphitheater sitting on a crate keeping out of the rain. She was writing again…but what? Nervously he walked over to her and pulled up another crate beside her as he tried to talk to her,

"What are you writing about?"

"Life." She answered.

"I'll take you home so you won't get so wet as soon as you're ready." He informed her.

"I can walk." She answered.

"I can wait." He insisted, not giving her a choice.

Sonny felt giddy just sitting by her, he couldn't drive clear to her home, but he could get her close.

"You got Wiley's truck, huh? How'd you manage that?" Pam asked.

"I'm doing some work for him, and he felt I needed wheels. He also got me a cell phone to keep in contact with him, give me your pen and I'll write down my number." Sonny suggested, sort of hoping he could see a bit of what she was writing.

"Just give me the number and I'll write it down." She answered back.

Well it was a good try anyway. He thought to himself.

"So, you're doing the Boss Work on the Casa's." Pam stated matter-of-factly.

Sonny was a bit surprised as he said she was right.

"I know almost everything going on in this town," she added, "what do you think of Homer's plans?"

Shocked again at her knowledge he replied, "They look great."

He finally mustered up the courage to ask her point blank, "Why are you always journalizing - and what are you writing?"

"Life," she answered as she did before, "just life."

Well, that had gotten him nowhere so he decided to just sit by her until she was ready to go home. Sitting quietly by her was very nice.

About an hour later the rain let up, and she was ready to go home, so Sonny walked her to the pickup and opened the door.

"You've got it all cleaned up inside, now I'm going to get it all muddy." Pam told him.

"That's ok, Pam," he assured her, "I don't mind cleaning up after you…I mean I can clean up your mud…I mean…"

"Sonny," Pam cut in realizing he was a bit flustered, which really amused her, "it's okay, and you'll clean it up."

He wasn't sure what – or if – he should say anything else on the way to her corner where he would drop her off and then head home.

When Sonny pulled into the *Rainrest Motel,* no cars were there, so he knew they had no guests again. His mom and dad would not be happy when they called. As he walked in his sister took off for her room without a word to him. He sure wishes she wouldn't do that. He knows how utterly lonely she is not letting him or anyone into her space.

He sat down at the computer to surf and study, but his mind couldn't get off Pam and her book of writings. Partly because she is so beautiful she makes his heart flutter, and partly because his curiosity was really getting to him.

Sonny Boatright has never been short on curiosity or imagination.

Thoughts of an old machine in the storeroom at the back of the motel kept coming to mind, he didn't know why. He had seen a rather large machine back there loaded with junk like old lamps, broken chairs and motel furniture of various kinds. He didn't know what the machine was, but he felt lead to check it out.

As he sat 'junk' out in the hall, his sister heard him rummaging around and darted into the room and grabbed a good-sized plastic box and ran back to her room locking the door behind her.

Peculiar. He thought to himself, but then went on about his work.

There was the machine, and as he unloaded the odd lampshades and curtains off of it he could see part of a name on it – St—d—rd. There were also the remnants of a telephone number starting with 800. He saw a small label under the name that had four colored strips on it. It was a large old printer.

"Wow!" He exclaimed right out loud as he started inching it toward the hallway.

It was really heavy and he had to rock it from side to side to move it. It took him almost an hour to *walk* it out into the hall.

As he lifted the lid and saw it had a large glass area, "Gosh," he mumbled to himself, "this is for big printing. That table must be over eighteen inches wide and twenty-four inches long. Wonder what they used to print on this?"

He found three trays in the two doors on the bottom of the machine; one was for letter size paper, one for eleven by seventeen and one without markings - for just plain big. He figured the oversized paper might have been for printing up legal forms.

The grey electrical cord did not have the three prongs for safety; the grounding one was missing.

"I can get an adapter and screw it to the wall, and that will ground it all right," he said to himself, "until I can get a new heavy duty – grounded – cord hooked up."

The big printing machine was really dirty, and he didn't know how long it had been there. The *Rainrest Motel* had been there for over forty years, and it almost looked like the old machine came with it. He knew it was a four-color machine by the four colored bars under the partial nameplate.

Not knowing much about printing machines, he decided to go on the Web and see what he could find out about printers.

Especially old machines. But first – the cleaning with Fantastic; and possibly Comet. Then he would plug it in and see what was needed to make it work. All of the fine parts seemed in order as he opened up the back. The ink cartridges were empty, but he could see the re-order numbers. The inside looked great; he figured it must have a good seal on the door.

    On his way back to the office, he tapped on his sister's door as he passed it, but she didn't respond. It seemed like they were each living alone.

Seven Baptisms

When the seven who were to be baptized walked into church, Elder Barstow showed each one to the front row. The second row was roped off for family members of the seven.

Kelli had slipped in and was sitting behind Todd. She touched his shoulder as he sat down, and he turned around and smiled at her. Todd could see his two brothers, Ira and Billy, sitting in the very back row – with Sonny.

Sheriff Leo and Deputy Homer had even stepped into the back of the church; they wouldn't miss seeing Todd Carson baptized. Jake was sitting on the outside aisle in the same row that the sheriff was sitting in. But strangely – he had sent Angela to sit up behind Wiley. Deputy Homer was sitting across the aisle from Leo. Leo and Homer were also armed.

Then a really strange thing happened, Sonny thought, Jani came in and started to stop and talk to Homer – but he shooed her away and told her to go sit by Angela – NOW! He had never used that authoritarian voice with her before and she was a bit dumbfounded. She looked over at Jake and he nodded his head to go sit with Angela too.

Dad Judd walked in – no one had expected him to be there, and he went up and sat down between Jani and Angela.

Sonny wondered if he was the only one smelling something in the 'air', and seeing things he knew were out of the ordinary. Then Pam walked in and sat on the other side of the church so she could see almost everything.

As he stood up, Ira said "Easy boy", and Sonny glanced at him as he moved on up to the outside of the row Pam was sitting in.

Now Sonny was sure something was strange. Jake, John Judd, Ira, Leo and Homer were all up to something.

Kelli was beaming with pride; now they wouldn't be unequally yoked should she decide to tell Todd how she feels.

Wiley and Wilson were sitting behind Annabelle and Wayne; she had her hand up on her shoulder as Wiley held it with one hand while he had his other hand on Wayne's shoulder.

Nancy and Henry Pepper were the new couple, and no one knows anything about them yet. If Pastor John does – he isn't telling.

Sonny couldn't help but notice that Jake seemed particularly interested in the new couple, and was constantly scanning the congregation. His guts were telling him something is not as it seems, especially since he could see a big bulge in Jake's boot.

The older gentleman is sixty-nine-year old Austin Downs, and the young lady is fifteen-year old Courtney Bingham; both *Woods People*.

As Pastor John finished the short Sunday evening sermon, he announced that there were seven new Christians that want to make their public confession of faith in Jesus Christ, and everyone was welcome to stay and witness the celebration.

"Let us pray." Pastor John started.

"Welcome to each of you in the name of our Lord Jesus Christ." He said to the seven as he stepped down from the podium to talk directly to them.

Elder Barstow and Wiley opened the Baptistery after they removed the pulpit.

Pastor John continued talking directly to the seven, "You are all here this evening to proclaim to the public your commitment to, and faith in our Savior. Do you each know what you are committing to? You are committing to follow Jesus Christ…no matter what!

"In the Bible, in *Mark, Chapter ten,* Christ Jesus asked the people, 'Do you know what you are asking for? Are you prepared to drink from the cup that I drink from?' Our Lord knew that a commitment to Him and to the Christian life would not be an easy task then, and it will certainly not be easy now. In our world Christians are not always treated well. Often times we are mocked and laughed at. We must pledge to stand fast.

"For those of us who are serious about our Commitment to Christ our Lord, in the twenty-eighth chapter of *Matthew* and in the sixteenth chapter of *Mark* we are commanded to be baptized *'to complete all righteousness.'* Please take time to read both of these chapters in God's Word, our Bible. The Bible is God's actual letter to us, just as we write to others.

"I ask each of you, right now…are you sure you want to commit to walking with Christ Jesus as a Christian, and make a public confession to this commitment by being baptized? Think about it for a moment.

"Now, raise your right hand if you are freely choosing to follow Jesus Christ…no matter what Satan may throw at you. You do realize Satan is mad at you, don't you? He is right now acting like a roaring lion, and would give anything to devour you and get you back. Ephesians Chapter Four, verse twenty-seven tells us not to give the devil an opportunity. Keep your eyes on Christ and not on your circumstances, and God will work everything out for you – according to His plan for your life. God does have a plan for each one of you – in His timing, not yours.

"You must put faith in action by keeping your eyes on Christ first, and then everything else will follow. Circumstances always change – always – but God never changes. *Hebrews* thirteen, verse eight - says, *Jesus Christ is the same yesterday, today, yes and forever.* Also read verse nine telling you not to be carried away by varied and strange teachings. Get into God's letter to you, the Bible. Listen to what He is saying to you.

"*Matthew* three, verse two, tells us that repentance is a change of mind that bears fruit in a changed life. You have all repented of your sins; that is why you are here tonight…to make public your own confession of Christ coming into your lives – and of your changed lives. You will still have hard times, but remember – it doesn't matter what you like or dislike – it's what is right and wrong.

"We see in *First Peter,* the third chapter that water itself cannot save you. Water baptism is the open confession of your changed life, a life that has a conscience that is at peace with God Almighty – through faith in Jesus Christ.

"*Mark* chapter one and verse four says the Apostle John immersed converts as a witness to their repentance – and in the name of The Father, The Son and the Holy Spirit, as a witness to their faith in Christ Jesus. Your faith in Christ and Him crucified for all your sins is all that matters now – you don't have to do anything else – just have faith that you have justification in Christ and Christ alone.

"Baptism, as told in *Romans* the sixth chapter, separates us from our old lives, and enters us into our new life. We are no longer cursed by Adam's sin, but we are now in Christ and our baptism is a reminder of this. When we are buried with Christ in Baptism, we are now in the likeness of His death, and now also we are entitled to be in Christ in the likeness of His Resurrection.

"In other words, when we are buried with Christ in baptism, we will also be raised up with Him through faith. We are putting off our old person, and putting on our new person. You have died to sin's control over you.

"Not that you will never sin again, because everyone does… but you can confess it…and be forgiven…and go on. Christians aren't perfect, just forgiven.

"In *Matthew* chapter ten and verse thirty-two Jesus tells us that if we will confess Christ before man, Christ will confess us before His Father in Heaven. You need to tell people of Christ. Remember also…the only thing you can take to Heaven with you… is someone else…IF you have witnessed to them and they have accepted Christ Jesus.

"When we are justified by faith in Christ, we will have peace with God through our Lord Jesus Christ.

"This Baptism today is your solemn commitment to follow The Lord, no matter what happens. May God bless each of you, and give you Grace, Peace and Strength to stand up to the anger of Satan, and the courage to get into God's Word to us...the Bible... and to not be partakers with the Sons of Disobedience."

Elder Barstow had already stepped down into the baptistery and was waiting for the pastor to join him.

Emily lined up the seven on the stage, starting with the ladies.

Annabelle was the first to step down in the water as Pastor John took her hand to keep her from falling. Wiley was there with the camera; he was going to get pictures of everyone for Pastor John and of Annabelle and Wayne for himself.

"Annabelle Close," Pastor was saying, "by your own repentance of your sin, and your commitment to Christ and His cross, I baptize you in the name of the Father, the Son and the Holy Ghost and into the Lord Jesus Christ."

Then Pastor Stoddard and Elder Barstow dipped Annabelle under the water and brought up the new creature in Christ. Emily and Mia were waiting at the end with a warm towel for her, and for each one after her.

One by one each of the rest of the seven made their public confession to Christ, Nancy, Courtney, Austin, Todd and Wayne.

As Wayne came up out of the water, Wiley grabbed Wayne's towel and was holding it open to receive his boy. He wrapped the towel around Wayne and hugged him.   He sure wanted to hug Annabelle too, but didn't think that was a good idea.

"Let's all give the Lord a *praise offering* for our new family members." Pastor John announced as he and Barstow climbed up out of the tank into waiting towels.

Everyone stood up and clapped as the new members of the family of God and their families went to the changing rooms to dry off.

Jake was right behind them.

Then it was time for everyone to go to the kitchen to have hot chocolate and Mia's homemade Cross cookies.

It was a joyous day in *Raincroft*.

A City Trip & Ball Field Plans

Monday morning Barstow and Sonny headed for the City. They wanted to get the portable basketball hoops for practice tomorrow night.

"At least they will be able to shoot baskets," Barstow was saying, "I wonder what they've decided on for names for the other team. Naming their opponents is hilarious Sonny, you're so remarkable, and what an imagination."

"Yeah, and my imagination was really working last night at church; something was up, but I couldn't put my finger on it." Sonny stated quizzically...

Barstow didn't answer.

Sonny already had paper and pen in hand as they walked into the Athletics Complete store. Hank Thompson, the owner, greeted them. He already knew Barstow, but not the young man with him.

"Hank, this is Sonny Boatright, he's my associate." Barstow announced.

"Hello, Sonny," Hank responded, "good to meet you. What can I help you gentlemen with today?"

Sonny's heart was dancing around saying, *I'm a gentleman, I'm a gentleman.*

The happy young man handed Hank the list he had created of things he knew they would need for the permanent ball field; hoops, backboards, nets, scoreboards and uniforms. They would need to be labeled and numbered.

"If you have a copy machine, I'll leave you this list. Please find us your best price on each item and call me." Sonny grinned as he gave Hank his cell number.

Hank looked at Barstow who smiled at him and nodded. Evidently Sonny could speak for Barstow, - who knew the young man had experience ordering things for the *Rainrest Motel.*

Hank disappeared to the back of the store, then came back with a photocopy of the list and handed it to Sonny.

"Now we need two of those portable hoops for temporary use and six good regulation size basketballs to take today." Barstow told Hank.

Sonny looked at the prices, "Whew, Hank, these are pretty expensive. Since we're going to be doing several hundred dollars' worth of purchasing, what kind of a special can you do for us?"

Barstow was chuckling at his young businessman.

"Well, they are already marked down to rock bottom price, Sonny," Hank was saying, "see here is the original price, and this is the sale price."

"Not good enough," Sonny responded, "we have to have a cheaper price than that or we will go to the *Boundaries Game Store.* I'm sure with the amount of business we are needing to do they will be more cooperative."

With that he nodded at Barstow to go.

Hank hollered at them, "Wait, stop, I'll give the hoops to you for exactly my cost."

"And the balls." Sonny replied.

After a couple of deep breaths Hank said, "Yes, the balls too."

As Sonny went over to check out which balls have the highest ratings, Hank asked Barstow, "Where'd you get this kid? Does he need a job?"

"God brought him to us the hard way," Barstow chuckled, "and he sure does not need another job."

Hank looked puzzled at the hard way comment, but didn't inquire further.

On the way back to *Raincroft,* Barstow was congratulating

Sonny for how he handled the purchase, and for how much money he had saved him. Bickering prices was right up Sonny's alley; he was obviously having a ball himself.

The team was all present and accounted for. Sonny had set up the hoops on the concrete in front of the amphitheater since Mayor Roscoe said he could. Deputy Homer was front and center checking things out.

Jake, Wiley, and Barstow had taken seats on the front step of the amphitheater ready for the meeting, and Sonny joined them as Homer began to speak,

"Ok, fellas, what have you decided for your opponents' team's name and their colors? Let's start with Ronnie, what's your team's choice for Wiley's team?"

"We've unanimously named them the *Electrics* and their colors will be red and white." Ronnie answered for Homer's Team.

"Good name; good colors," Homer congratulated his team. "Now, who will speak for Wiley's team?"

Jimmy stood up and said, "We've decided on calling Wiley's team the Thunders, and they'll wear blue and white."

"Very, very good." Homer remarked.

The four men sitting on the bottom step started smirking.

"Looks like we've had some collusion here." Jake remarked.

Wiley and Homer picked four from each of their teams to lead off the practices. The balls bounced much better on the concrete, and the portable hoops were great. The kids were having a ball throwing the balls, even though they missed most of the baskets. That didn't matter, - this was for fun.

The deputy let the first four practice about twenty minutes, then sent them back to the steps and called the remaining five from each team out to practice. Twenty minutes later he sent them to the bench.

The five men were watching the moves of each kid to determine what position they were most suited for. Sure, this was for fun, but it still had to have a measure of competition to keep their interests.

"Now, I will have the balls in my office, an' you cain come an' sign them out as long as you sign them back in." Homer told the boys, "You must never throw the balls at anyone; if you do you'll be out of the game. There won' be no game this Saturday 'cause of Angela and Jake's weddin'."

Looking over at the four men sitting on the step Homer asked them, "Got anything you wan' to say?"

All four men shook their heads no, as Barstow pointed to the galvanized tub and treat box.

"You all are dismissed to the treats." Homer slowly shouted to the kids.

"You're talking even better, Deputy," Jake said to him on the way over to the office for another planning meeting.

"Been practicin' my ABC's, and on two words a day. Like today is to and you. G's is harder, an' sometimes not heard, like H's. D's is also hard." The deputy responded.

Barstow started going over the copy of the list that Sonny had made up.

"I tell you guys something," Barstow elaborated, "if you want to save money, take this young businessman with you. I really enjoyed watching him make Hank squirm with his coercing. He saved us approximately two-hundred-fifty dollars getting things at cost. He even threatened Hank with us going to the Boundaries to get our sports supplies. It jarred Hank into compliance."

Everyone was congratulating Sonny, even Wiley's boys; especially Wilson.

Jake couldn't lay out the footings until after his honeymoon. Sonny said he'd get with Todd to draw up official Permit Plans to coincide with Deputy Homer's plans; if that was all right with everyone.

Sonny asked if he could take Ronnie Baker again, along with Chad Wall to measure the sole plates and start the wall studs on the Casas. Sonny also thought Wayne should go with him to learn the business. Everyone agreed, and so the morning was set.

"Can I call my mom and tell her we're on the way home?" Wayne asked when he got into the Jeep. He was obviously tired from his day as a carpenter's apprentice.

"You bet," the big man answered him, "but before we head home what shall we pick up to eat?"

"Pizza." Wayne's one-word answer came.

"You're a pizza." Wiley chuckled at his boy, "sounds good as long as you eat your salad too."

Jake's cell rang, and he figured it was his lady, so he smartly answered without checking the Caller I.D., "I love you my little sweetie."

"I love you too, but I'm not your sweetie." Ira's deep voice came back.

"All right, all right," Jake responded, "everything ok?"

"Sure is, little sweetie," Ira said mimicking, "meet me at Ernie's for a cup of coffee and I'll fill you in."

As the two mountain men sat down in the booth, Ira was all smiles.

"You look like a cat that just swallowed a bird, what's up." Jake asked his bro.

"As of July-first I am going to be a business owner–in training. I talked to Lenore and she and I have come to an Agreement. She does not want to sell the business to an outsider, and was actually waiting for me to come and see her. She gave me a complete Accounting Course I have to give to Mam. I couldn't believe it when she said she and Mam had been talking about me. My ears weren't even ringing.

I start Monday morning learning the computer, English, Grammar and Accounting. I guess Little Joe's got the computers finished in the Family Room. I'll just park at the turn-a-round and walk up the path, and that's certainly no problem. I have the remote in my pocket. I am so buzzed I can hardly sit still – I'm going to be making more money now than I was at Marks Mill. And I'll learn to not be so uncouth." Ira chattered. As he said uncouth his thoughts momentarily went into space.

Jake knew he was thinking about Leslie.

Ira filled his Bro in on Lenore's story and how she didn't need any money for anything; about how her husband had gone missing down in the canyon; and even about how the boy Wilson comes in and pretends he is an accountant at a little desk she keeps just for him. It's almost like she has a grandkid with her for a bit, and she really enjoys him. Her real grandkids are in New Mexico, where she will be retiring.

"Did you know, Jake," Ira continued, "she and her husband are both *Woods People?* I didn't know it. Lenore certainly has pulled herself up by the bootstraps and become successful. She even owns the building her office is in – and it goes with our deal. I really think I can become successful too."

"I know you can, Bro." Jake assured him.

Todd Visits Nelli & A Rehearsal

Will was just leaving to go check the mail when Todd's Toyota pulled into their driveway. Todd was happy to see Will leaving because he wanted to talk to Nelli alone.

"Kelli's not home." Will informed Todd.

Todd nodded; he hadn't wanted her there right then anyway.

Todd was there about thirty minutes, and was just leaving as Will returned home.

"What's so funny?" Will ask his mother noting the smirk on her face.

"Oh, nothing special, Todd is just so funny." She answered him.

The subject was dropped.

Thursday afternoon Jake picked up the lovely lady who was just hours away from being his wife. Angela looked particularly lovely to Jake as they greeted each other with warm hugs and delicious kisses.

"Two more days," she was purring, "an' we won' have to separate agin."

"I can hardly wait," he replied, "I'm counting the minutes. I dropped off the vows we made to Pastor John. We will be going over them with him before the rehearsal."

"Todd's picking up Kelli, and she's happy about that too." Angela told him as they were heading for the church.

"Has Kelli told Todd how she feels yet?" Jake inquired of Angela.

"No, she doesn't wanna be too forward an' scare 'im away." She replied.

"That's not likely." Jake chuckled as they pulled into the church parking lot.

"But she might soon, since they ar' not unequally yoked now." Angela continued.

Jake gazed at Angela; she was speaking slowly and carefully and pronouncing words he didn't know she could.

Jake noticed Sheriff Leo sneaking around behind the church watching things. The sheriff sure had latched onto something, and he felt it had something to do with the numerous break-ins around the area the last few months.

Pastor John had a list of questions for Jake and Angela, including where they want their *Unity Candles* located and do they want to be facing the audience, or have their backs to them. He also needed to know how they want the kneeling benches - side by side or facing each other?

After talking, they decided to face the audience to light the candles, and to be facing each other when they kneel for Communion. There were several other questions needing answered. It all took about an hour.

Barstow will take their list and set everything up as they want it to be.

They were still in the Pastor's office talking when the other guests started arriving. Josie, Beth, Mia and Emily went right downstairs to set up tables for the reception dinner. Barstow went to Pastor John's office to run through the things the bride and groom want.

The church already had white lace cloths that were perfect. Mam had Jani pick up a large roll of mint green plastic to put under the tablecloths and as the color poked through the lace, it looked regal. Josie would take the tablecloths home and launder them if anything got spilled during the rehearsal dinner.

Dad was taking photos of everything and everyone, especially Mam.

"Shouldn't you be saving the pictures for the wedding?" Josie asked her husband.

"No, I'm taking pictures of the prettiest lady in the town. If I run out of space, I'll just get another card...I already have one extra card." He assured her.

Josie smiled at her still amorous husband.

Jani and Carrie came down and were in a huddle with Jani's dad, soon Jess joined them. Josie and Emily were pretty sure they knew what was going on as they winked at each other – vehicle decorating.

Carrie went back upstairs to the piano to practice the processional music.

Billy Carson had shown up, he wasn't in the wedding, even though he would be looking after Orpha. He was sitting on the side of the church watching Carrie play. He and Sonny would be picking up Orpha and getting her to church, and then home again.

Jake had told Billy he could use the ATV, but Billy told him since Sonny had a truck now, and he and Sonny would have no problem loading her into the back after Pam and Carrie had her all dressed.

Both Billy and Pam would ride in the back of the truck with Orpha to keep her safe. That way she wouldn't be jostled around in a run-a-way wheel chair. Billy would push the chair to the corner to reach the truck, but that wouldn't be any problem with the healthy young man. In fact, if it wouldn't tolerate the ruts, he would probably just pick-up and carry the chair with her in it.

As each person took their place for the rehearsal, Angela headed for the basement to wait in the dressing room. Cindy and her associate were snapping pictures right and left.

When Angela saw Mam in the kitchen she ran over to her and hugged her as the two ladies chattered like jay-birds. Mam held her like the daughter she is becoming; Angela was so emotional that Mam thought she might be a nervous wreck by the wedding.

Soon Jani joined them.

"These kinds of nerves are why the bride and groom cannot see or talk to each other after midnight the day of the wedding. I know they are happy nerves, but they can also be a bit scary. You are becoming a full-fledged woman, leaving your youth behind. But, Honey, it's going to be exciting and wonderful, and Jani and I are here if you need anything." Mam encouraged her as she and Jani walked her to the dressing room.

First the Pastor, Jake and Jess came out of the Prayer Room and stood on the stage. Little Joe walked Josie up to sit down in the front row aisle seat, and dad and Jani followed. Then Will pretended to wheel Orpha's chair down to the front and put it in the space where Barstow had removed the small bench. Pam followed him to sit by Orpha and be sure she was all right so Angela wouldn't have to worry about her mother.

Then came Kelli walking by herself – and Todd was grinning as he watched her graceful figure glide down the aisle. Kelli was grinning at Todd too, as she kept thinking he looked like he was up to something. Having been around each other since kindergarten they could almost read each other's minds.

As Carrie started the *Bridal March* song, everyone stood up, and Angela started walking up to the front of the church with her brother on her right arm. She was crying even though it is just a rehearsal, and Jake started crying too as he seen his very soon to be wife coming to him. He stepped out beside Mike.

The rehearsal was without error. Everyone knew what he/she was to do, and did it flawlessly. The only hitch was the bride and groom having a hard time talking through their tears, and even though it isn't in the program, Jake took Angela and held her to comfort her as she cried.

As Todd sang a few words from both of their love songs, he and Kelli were also in tears. Dad Judd was hoping with all the weeping tonight, that Saturday there would be a little more cured. Not at all because weeping is bad, but because it might ruin the make-up on the beautiful ladies' faces for pictures. As he looked over at is lovely wife, she also was weeping – and so was Jani – and so was Carrie – and so was Emily - and so was Mia - and so was

Pam – and so was…Tears, tears, tears, everywhere, and it's just the rehearsal.

Billy was heading for the door to leave when Jake hollered at him to wait, and invited him to please join them for dinner, there was plenty. Billy looked over at Todd, and his big brother nodded affirmatively at him. Ira also gave him a nod. Jake insisted that his 'bro' Ira be there for the dinner. Both of the Carson boys were very much a part of the wedding party. Ira was helping Sarah and picking up and distributing flowers, and Billy was looking after the mother of the bride. Jake also nodded at Sonny to join them; he also will be looking after Orpha.

Jake and Angela sat at the head of the table and didn't seem to remember that there were others at the table; they were so engrossed with each other. Jake had almost forgotten he was supposed to eat; he was feasting on this woman beside him.

Todd had grabbed a seat by Kelli, who almost seemed to be saving it for him.

Jake would be coming with his parents in the GMC. Mam would have to ride in the back with Jani because Jakes long legs wouldn't fit in the king cab. Unc and Little Joe would be bringing the ATV and Jess would pick up Beth.

Tomorrow all clothes would be brought to church for the bridal party. As soon as the groom and best man were dressed Saturday, they would go and wait in the Prayer Room on the opposite side of the stage from the Pastor's Study until the Pastor came and beckoned them it was time to start.

Angela and Kelli would wait in the ladies dressing room with Mam and Jani. Carrie would start playing the piano about eleven thirty so people could enjoy the music as they entered and were seated by Will and Joe. Jake did not want any division; such as this is the Bride's side and this is the Groom's side. The seating would start from the front and work back.

Jake and Angela had decided to not see each other on Friday, even though they could talk on the phone. With emotions so out of control and so much they each had to do, they thought a day to just get things together would be a good idea. Jake had to pack for the honeymoon, Angela didn't have much to pack, and it had been done weeks ago. Her very soon to be husband had given her the money to buy a trousseau for the honeymoon; which he hadn't been able to see yet. All he had seen was the lovely pink suitcase holding the secret items.

The ATV went very slowly on the way home, as his woman squeezed his hand over and over. When he pulled into her driveway, they didn't go right inside; they decided to take a walk in the woods. It was dark so Jake kept his arm tight about her waist so if she fell he would catch her. It was so good to be able to hold her with two arms now. His arm was still a bit stiff from lack of use, but she seemed to want to be even closer to him, so he picked her up and cradled her in his arms as he sat down on a large rock. The very rock he had held her on so many times before. This would be the last time he would hold her as a girlfriend, the next time it would be as his wife.

Their hearts were beating totally in sync as they held each other close, talking about the upcoming events. Jake intended for these feelings to never leave their marriage, and as Dad had said, it's pretty much up to him to be sure she stays this cuddly.

"I love you with everything in me, Angela, and my commitment to you is real and forever. I will always take care of you." He told her as he kept kissing her sweet lips, then her forehead, her chin, the end of her nose, and then her neck.

"Me too." She responded between kisses.

To leave her tonight will be the hardest thing he has ever done. In just about thirty-six hours she would be his wife and his heart was beyond happy.

Jake and Angela's Wedding

The bride was in the ladies dressing room with her bridesmaid Kelli, along with Mam, Jani, Emily and Mia as Carrie started playing at eleven thirty sharp.

Angela was gushing, "One-half hour and I'll be Jake's wife. Mrs. Jake Judd."

Everyone was in a fervor. Jakes little red head would officially be a Judd in a little over thirty minutes.

Jake and Jess were now in the Prayer Room; dressed and ready to go.

Homer was one of the firsts to show up; he would be on duty to be sure everything went well. He was dressed in full uniform, all very neatly pressed. He had acquired a bottle of Drakkar.

Jani had to make a trip upstairs for an item. She paused as she passed him on the steps, and she couldn't help but notice how much Homer had grown up and how really nice he smelled.

Homer had paused too as he descended the steps. As their eyes met, they both grinned.

She had noticed him sniffing her out of the corner of her eye at the birthday party. He didn't know she had seen him – he forgot that she is a Judd too, and part wolf. But this time she was sniffing him.

"Wow, you smell great, Homer." Jani cooed giving him the once over.

"Thanks, Miss Jani, you look beautiful an' you smell good too." He might have gotten on the word slide, but someone coming down the steps interrupted them.

As people were arriving, Will and Joe were seating them. Unc was at the Guest Book, and hopefully he would remember to stay there.

The Wiley Roscoe family were some of the first to arrive; they wanted up close to the front so they could hear. Annabelle was gorgeous in her royal blue gown and white pearls. The guys looked so handsome in their matching suits, royal blue bow ties and handkerchiefs.

Will was telling Annabelle as she held on his arm on the way to be seated, "You are not supposed to be more beautiful than the bride." She giggled.

Annabelle had never thought of herself as being beautiful, and it made her giddy. The boys, and Wiley, were grinning ear to ear with pride. Wiley had gotten her a really lovely corsage with miniature white roses and blue carnations; he had even gotten blue carnations for his boys and himself. As the family sat down, both boys wanted the end of the pew to see Angela better, so Wiley told them that one of them could sit in the pew in front of the other one. Wayne said he would sit in front by himself since he's the oldest and didn't need to stay right with mom.

The sanctuary filled up fast, and everyone was commenting on how lovely the church was decorated. Jess and crew had done a good job.

There were large white bows on each pew end on both sides up the center aisle, and each one had a green carnation and white rose. They had also put matching bows and flowers on the unity candle table, on the two brass floor candelabras candles that stair-stepped up and on the kneeler benches.

The ushers would be lighting the floor candles and the two outside candles on the Unity Table just before the mothers took their places. Everything looked like a Royal Wedding.

Eleven-fifty-five and the ushers went up on stage and lit the candles. Pastor John tapped on the Prayer Room door and Jake and Jess came out and followed him to their assigned places.

The music got a bit louder as Little Joe walked his mother up to the front row on the left, and Jani followed on Dads arm. Josie almost looked angelic in her powder blue suit.

Once they were seated, Will pushed Orpha's decorated wheel chair up to her respective place, and Pam followed and sat down beside her on the right. The chair had white ribbon laced through the spokes, with mint carnations and white roses. Her right arm was going wild.

Pam noticed Sonny had taken a seat in the same row at the end by the wall; he sure looked dashing in his suit. She'd never seen him dressed up before.

Orpha's dress Velcro was a winner, she looked lovely. Mam had been right – again. Both mothers had their corsages on.

Nelli and Walter had come in – surprising everyone. Nelli had a corsage that matched the bridal bouquets, and Walter had a mint carnation in his lapel. They sat on the very last row on the aisle.

No one noticed the older scruffy looking man in the back corner.

Todd was at the piano and had taken a Mic. When everyone was seated, Carrie changed to a processional song, and here came Kelli up the aisle. She was stunning, and Todd wasn't sure he would be able to sing with the big lump in his throat. She slightly tripped as she was staring in his eyes. The sparks were flying as they grinned at each other. Todd couldn't believe her emerald satin gown was so perfect for her, with the white beads, and the matching shoes, she really looked like a princess.

Jess met her at the bottom step and took her arm to help her up the steps and to her place. Then he went back over and stood by his brother.

The Wedding March started, and everyone stood up, and there in the foyer on the way to meet her love was Angela, holding her brother Mike's left arm. Her gown was streaming behind her. The crystal tiara resting on the red hair was sparkling, and her veil was down over her face. Jake almost passed out as she got closer to the front of the church, he was so overjoyed.

As the Bride and Groom stood staring at each other, Todd started singing *"I only have eyes for you."*

Jess finally nudged Jake, to get him back to the Program, and

Jake stepped down beside Mike as Pastor John asked, "If there be anyone who has ought against this marriage, speak now, or forever hold your tongue."

No one said anything, and then the Pastor continued, "Who giveth this woman to be married to this man?"

"I, her brother, and her family do." Mike responded as he took his sister's hand and placed it in Jakes.

Jake could feel Angela was trembling as he squeezed her hand, to tell her everything is all right.

"Let us pray," Pastor continued, "Gracious Heavenly Father, we come to you in the precious name of Jesus Christ, and ask your blessing on this service, and on Jake and Angela's marriage. Amen.

Congregation, you may be seated."

The Pastor started the ceremony as Jake and Angela stared at each other. "Dearly beloved family and friends, we are gathered here today to witness the commitment of Jake and Angela to each other and to Almighty God. In Genesis, Matthew, Mark and Colossians, the Bible tells us that it is not good for man to be alone, that God Himself made male and female to live together under a covenant with each other, and with God, and how they are to treat each other.

In *Matthew* we are told *"That a man shall leave his mother and father and be united to his wife, and the two shall become one flesh. They will no longer be two people, but only one in Jesus Christ"*.

"So, I charge you both, Jake Judd and Angela Crabtree, before God and these witnesses gathered here to remember you are God's chosen people, holy and dearly loved, and grafted into His Eternal Presence. You must each clothe yourselves with compassion, kindness, humility, gentleness and patience toward each other. You must bear with each other and forgive whatever grievance you may have against one another. You must forgive as the Lord has forgiven you. Over all these virtues you must put on love, which binds all together in perfect unity. Let the peace of Christ rule in your hearts, since as members of one body you are called to peace.

"Be thankful. Let the Word of Christ dwell in you richly as

you teach and admonish one another with all wisdom. Sing to each other the Psalms, hymns and spiritual songs, with gratitude in your hearts to God for giving you to each other.

"Whatever you do, whether in word or deed, do all in the name of our Lord Jesus Christ; giving thanks to God the Father through Him. You must always keep Christ the center of your marriage. You must remember that your bodies will now belong to each other and that you are responsible to see that each is well cared for.

"When a choice must be made, you must always choose on the side of your marriage because it is a three-fold Unity, you Jake, you Angela and God Almighty. It is a three-fold cord that can never be broken. Your first allegiance is to God, and then each other. Never let anyone or anything come between you. If you do you will be in a state of sin.

"Always speak well of each other, for in doing so you will be keeping God's Commandments.

"Now, Jake and Angela, will you please say your Pledges to each other?"

Angela handed Kelli her bouquet as Jake took a paper out of his pocket.

He started the vows saying, "I, Jake Judd, take you, Angela Crabtree, to be my lawfully wedded wife, my constant friend, my faithful partner and my love from this day forward. In the presence of God, our family and friends, I offer you my solemn vow to be your true and faithful partner in sickness and in health, in good times and in bad times, in joy as well as in sorrow. I promise God and you that I will love you unconditionally, support you in your goals, honor and respect you. I will laugh with you, and cry with you. I will care for and cherish you for as long as I live, so help me God."

Angela took the Pledge paper from Jake as she repeated, "I, Angela Crabtree, take you, Jake Judd, to be my lawfully wedded husband, my constant friend, my faithful partner and my love from this day forward. In the presence of God, our family and friends I offer you my solemn vow to be your true and faithful partner in sickness and in health, in good times and in bad, in joy as well as sorrow. I promise God and you that I will love you unconditionally, support you in your goals, honor and respect you. I will laugh with you, and cry with you. I will care for and cherish you for as long as I live, so help me God."

Jake was amazed at how correctly Angela was reading the vows. Mam had been helping her to learn to speak the vows correctly - and she did.

"The rings please." Pastor John held up the rings as he continued, "These are golden rings. This precious metal symbolizes that your love is your most precious element in life. The ring has no beginning and no ending. This symbolizes that the love between you will never cease.

"Jake, please place the ring on Angela's finger as you repeat after me, "Angela, with this ring, I thee wed, and with it I bestow upon thee all the treasures of my mind, heart and hands. I am consecrated unto you according to the Law of Almighty God. Angela, will you take this ring as a symbol of my covenant?""

"I will," She answered, as Jake put the ring on her finger.

"Angela, please place the ring on Jake's finger as you repeat after me, "With this ring I thee wed, and with it, I bestow upon thee all the treasures of my mind, heart and hands. I am consecrated unto you according to the Law of Almighty God. Jake will you take this ring as a symbol of my covenant?""

"I will," He answered as she pushed the ring on Jakes finger.

Pastor John continued, "And now by your giving and receiving each other's pledges, and the exchanging rings, by the authority of the State of California, I now pronounce you are husband and wife. What God has joined together, let no man put asunder. You may now kiss your wife."

"I love you Mrs. Judd." Jake whispered as he raised her veil, "I wanted to be the first one to call you Mrs. Judd."

Todd started singing, 'In The Name Of The Father' as Jake kissed his now wife, and they stood there holding hands and gazing at each other until Todd finished the song.

Jake led his wife over to the *Unity Candle* where they each took an outside candle and lit the Unity Candle together. Then they extinguished the single candles signifying they are no longer two, but one flesh.

They went to the communion kneeling bench, and after Jake helped his wife kneel he went to the other side to kneel facing her.

As Pastor John picked up the small glass bowl, and the bride and groom each took a wafer, Pastor said, "As the first act of their marriage, Jake and Angela will take Communion. We will do this most holy act according to *First Corinthians 11:23-27, The Lord Jesus took bread, and when He had given thanks, He brake it, and said, "Take, eat: this is My Body, which is broken for you: this do in remembrance of Me.""*

The bride and groom each ate the wafer symbolizing the Body of Christ.

The Pastor picked up the two small glasses, and handed one to each as he continued: "After the same manner also He took the cup, when He had supped, saying, *"This cup is the New Testament in My Blood: this do ye, as oft as ye drink it, in remembrance of Me. For as often as ye eat this bread, and drink this cup ye do show the Lord's death till He comes again.""*

After Jake and Angela drank the cup, the Pastor prayed again. Then Jake helped his wife stand up, and they faced each other holding hands as Todd started singing their second love song,

"You Are So Beautiful To Me."

Angela took back her bouquet from Kelli as Todd finished their song and Pastor John said to the congregation, "I charge each one of you to support this couple by the commandments of God. Do you all accept this charge?"

The audience all agreed.

Then Pastor said, "I now present to you Mr. & Mrs. Jake Judd."

The newlyweds walked hand in hand down the steps and to the back foyer to wait in the receiving line. Jess and Kelli followed them and Todd was right behind them. Carrie kept playing soft music as the guests either left or headed down-stairs to the reception.

It seemed like the guests stopping to wish them the best would never end. Jake had caught a glimpse of a young lady with a black hat on and a veil covering her face. She had appeared in the back door, and left as soon as the ceremony was over.

Since Angela's train was so long, Zoe knew she couldn't loop it over her wrist, and had put three buttons at the waistline so the train could be bustled in back, keeping it off the floor completely. Kelli pulled the train up and was buttoning it into the bustle when she glanced up at Todd; he had cow eyes as he smiled at her. She was still wondering what he was up to as Angela and Jake descended the stairs into the reception hall.

It was a beautiful Reception. The cake had come out perfect.

As the newlyweds cut pieces of cake from the second tier and fed it to each other, flashes were going off like mad. Some of the cake dropped into Jake's newly trimmed beard, and Angela was trying to clean it for him. Everyone started laughing.

Everyone got glasses full of Sparkling Cider for the toast. As Jake and Angela wrapped their arms around each other's to drink everyone started clapping. Each time the guests started tapping their forks on their glasses, it meant for the bride and groom to kiss, and they happily obliged their guests.

The newlyweds went to the gift table to start opening the gifts. Mia was already taking the cake top off the cake and putting it in the freezer box.

Todd had grabbed the Guest Book from the table, since everyone else seemed to forget about it. He handed it to Kelli and she started writing down the gifts received by the name of each guest. Jess was supposed to bring it down, but he seemed to have other things on his mind – like Beth, she was beautiful in her powder blue gown and satin slippers. Her hair was in a French braid, and it had tiny white and blue flowers embedded in the cords of hair.

Mia, Beth and Emily were serving the cake to the guests, and somehow Barstow ended up dishing out the drinks.

Mam was supposed to help serve, but Angela wanted her right there with her at the gift table. If she would move away a bit to keep out of pictures, Angela would pull her right back; she wanted her new mom with her in the pictures. Sonny and Billy had picked up Orpha's chair and carried it downstairs so she could be in the pictures too, and enjoy the festivities.

Mia handed Wayne and Wilson sacks, and they were neatly folding the wrapping paper and putting it in them. Annabelle was receiving the bows from the packages. She wasn't sure what to do with all of them, so she just stood there holding them. They were now lining her arms, and she was beginning to look like a ribbon rack. Wiley started collecting some bows because they were starting to fall on the floor. The boys both had funny looks on their faces as they watched Wiley helping their mom, he even put his arm around her waist.

As Carrie and Pam stood by Orpha, Sonny stood by Pam, and Billy by Carrie, Jake made more mental notes.

The newlyweds received lots of cards with money, and many gift cards. Angela loved the gift cards; she could go shopping with Mam, Kelli and Jani.

The gifts were all open, and Mam had laid them out for everyone to see. Now for the bouquet.

"All the single girls get ready for the bouquet toss." Jess hollered as he handed Angela the toss bouquet.

There were about fifteen young ladies in the group as Angela tossed her flowers over her head backwards. Beth wasn't participating in the toss, but the lovely bouquet came right at her, and she caught it to keep it from hitting her face.

"Okay guys," Jake hollered, "time for the garter toss."

There were about twenty single men in their group.

As Jake pulled the garter off of his wife's leg with his teeth, she kept giggling, his beard was tickling her. It took him a bit to get his teeth gripped on the garter because he was laughing so hard, and everyone was going wild. Finally, as it slid down over her foot Jake quickly covered her leg with her dress. Then he stretched it and shot it backward to the fellas.

Mike Crabtree caught the garter. Everyone was saying that Mike doesn't even have a girlfriend, and he was leaving in the morning for the Air Force, Billy Carson would use Ira's truck to take him to the City Airport. Jake seemed pleased that Angela's brother caught her garter. He wasn't too savvy with another male having one of her private articles.

Billy was kind of hoping Carrie could ride with them, but he knew she had to stay with Orpha. Mike was insistent that he didn't want any party or going away fiasco. Mike likes things smooth and peaceful, and has always been sort of a loner.

Finally, the festivities were pretty much over, and it was time for Jake and his wife to take off, so they headed toward the stairs.

Be My Love Kelli

Just as the bride and groom were on the second stair in their leaving, Todd took the Mic off the reception table and asked for everyone's attention.

Jake and Angela stopped, and watch as Todd took a hold of Kelli's two hands and dropped to one knee.

"Kelli, I've loved you since you were in kindergarten and I was in first grade. Remember when I gave you that kiss on your cheek? I vowed then I would marry you. I don't have the money to put on this fancy wedding, but you couldn't look more gorgeous, and I already have a tuxedo on, and you already have a lovely bouquet.

"If Pastor John will perform the ceremony right now we can get the License Monday, I don't think that will matter time wise, we will be married in God's eyes. So, Kelli Armstrong, will you marry me right here and now? Jake and Angela can stand up with us." Todd asked Kelli with tears in his eyes.

Kelli was shocked, as was everyone else. She looked around to see the guest's expressions, including the bride and grooms - who were smiling.

"Todd, I've loved you too since you gave me that kiss on my cheek in kindergarten. I don't know how this is going to work out, but YES, I will marry you right now if Pastor John will marry us," she replied among her tears, "but what about rings?"

Todd reached into his pocket and pulled out a little gold box.

As he opened it Kelli could see two matching gold rings as she said, "How did you know my size?"

"Each time I was touching your soft fingers, I was measuring for your wedding ring." He replied.

There was electricity in the air with the love these two had shared for many years.

Todd stood up and they both turned to Pastor John Stoddard who nodded yes.

Angela came running back down the stairs to hug her friend as she said, "Yes, we'll stan' up with you. We always dreamed o' a double weddin' – now it's like we got a'r wishes. They ain't at the same tim', but they's still together. I'm so happy we've got an almost double weddin'. An' there's cake and drinks lef' for you all, and yu can use ar Unity Candles, and I know Pastor John has more Communion stuff, an'..."

Jake cut in and kissed his wonderful and compassionate bride. She had reverted to her old speech slides.

Todd Carson had always had to make things happen in his life if he wanted something. He worked hard, and wiggled around circumstances in silence, until they were like he wanted them. This was not an exception, now Kelli could have a beautiful wedding, and an almost double-wedding he had heard her talk about so often with her best friend Angela. Usually when she had no idea he was paying any attention to her, he was just busy fixing things around her.

Still a bit stunned Pastor John asked for everyone who was going to attend the new wedding to please go to the sanctuary without food in about fifteen minutes. Almost everyone wanted to join the surprise wedding.

Pastor John took Jake aside and asked him how he felt about what had happened. Jake was very happy with what was going on. He had always known too that the two girls wanted a double wedding. But since Todd didn't have any money for a nice wedding, he had put their relationship on hold. Jake has known how industrious Todd has been from childhood when he sets his mind on something.

"This will certainly make both ladies very happy, and that makes me happy." Jake told the pastor.

John asked Kelli and Todd to meet him in his study.

"Here is a copy of Jake and Angela's vows. They said you are very welcome to use them. You may read from them just like they did. Apparently, Todd, you have been planning this for a while." John remarked.

"Yes, Pastor John," Todd admitted, "I don't have the money to give this beautiful lady the wedding she deserves, and I knew that Kelli and Angela wanted a double wedding. We've been together for years, and I love her with everything in me. I knew Angela would be thrilled, and I know Jake is all right with us using his accessories too. It will be a long time before I can afford a wedding dress like the one Kelli has on. Isn't she breathtaking? Besides the old saying, married in green, you'll feel like a queen and that's how I'm going to treat her."

The lovebirds waited in the Pastor's office several minutes reading and doing a bit of rearranging the vows as Pastor went to finish preparations and talk with Emily.

Then the couple went to the foyer to wait for the music to start their wedding. Todd pulled a small Guest Book out of his jacket pocket and laid it on the stand in the foyer as he said to his soon-to-be-wife, "Hopefully a few guests will sign our book so we can read names together later."

Todd is an organized man. Mike was standing in the foyer, so Todd asked him if he would mind getting some signatures for him.

"Sure." Mike agreed.

The tiny figure appeared in the doorway of the foyer again. She still had the black hat and veil on. Mike said hello to her, but she didn't respond. She slipped up to the guest book and signed it, then stood over in the corner to watch. Mike moved slightly over in front of her to help keep her hidden and ignored her so she wouldn't run away.

The cameras were still running and Carrie was playing the piano. Will was standing by to sing a love song. Jake told Cindy to get pictures of Todd and Kelli too, and charge them to him, not Todd. That would be his and his wife's gift to the newlyweds.

As Todd and Kelli walked up the aisle together, Todd paused

at Nelli's row and took her arm so she could walk to the front of the church with them like a regular Mother of the Bride.

As he sat her down in the very front row, Kelli smiled and leaned over and kissed her mother on the forehead. Her mother's corsage matched her bridal bouquet. Kelli knew that this wonderful man, Todd Carson, had thought of everything, even a corsage for her mother and a carnation for her father.

Walter walked behind his wife sporting the green carnation in his lapel. Billy and Sonny had brought Orpha back upstairs. Her arm was really swinging; she was having the time of her life. Billy was pretty sure Orpha knew what had been going on that day. Billy and Orpha seem to have a special bond that has grown over the years. He talks to her as if she is his mom – since he hasn't had one.

Pastor John married Todd and Kelli with the same ceremony Jake and Angela had put together, with a few variances to make it their own.

Jake and Angela didn't stand one on each side of Todd and Kelli as you would expect. They stood together hand in hand as Jake and his wife listened to the words again, they were overwhelmed with love for each other, and with gratitude at how strangely the Lord does sometimes work.

After the ring part of the ceremony, Todd surprised Kelli by singing *""Be My Love""* to her instead of Will singing a song for them.

As he held her hands, and is deep baritone voice filled the church with heavenly music of love, everyone was in tears.

When the minister pronounced Todd and Kelli husband and wife and said, "You may now kiss your bride." Todd took his wife in his arms and for the first time kissed her the long sweet kiss he had been dreaming about for so many years.

Todd held his wife's hand as they walked over to the Unity Candle table together to extinguish their separate lives and light the emblem of their life beginning together. Then Todd helped his new wife kneel at the communion kneeling bench. Like Jake and Angela, they wanted to start their married life with the Lord in the center.

Todd wouldn't even let go of Kelli's hand for Communion;

it was as though he was afraid someone would take her away from him. The way she was smiling at him told his heart he had done a good thing, and his new wife is very happy.

Then as Pastor John presented, "Mr. & Mrs. Todd Carson." The newlyweds started the recessional and Todd leaned over and kissed Nelli on her forehead.

After a few more pictures of the second new bride and groom, Jake and Angela went outside of the church to leave and were bombarded with birdseed. It got in their hair, down their backs and even in their shoes. And, there was Angela's little turquoise tank all decorated.

To everyone's surprise, Jake loved it, and wanted pictures of them standing in front of it, behind it, and of him loading his wife into her little vehicle, after a few kisses. He also wanted pictures of their leaving in his wife's little turquoise tank – with her driving. Mam was crying as she and Dad Judd watched their two children drive away into their new life together.

Todd waited to talk to John Stoddard after all the congratulations and cake eating was over. He asked him about renting one of his empty cabins for a couple of months. Just until his *Casa* could be occupied.

"Absolutely, the cabin at the end in the woods is vacant, and I'll just leave the key stuck in the door lock so you can come home whenever you want to." John Stoddard assured him.

After the brief reception, Todd and Kelli went outside to get into the Toyota – low and behold – it was decorated too. And, there was a card from Ernie and Eva Caldwell on the windshield telling Mr. & Mrs. Todd Carson to please be their guests for their wedding supper tonight at the *Canyon Steak Corral.*

"I talked to Billy and Mike during the reception, and they will be taking Orpha home in Sonny's pick-up, it worked fine on the way over. He thought Pam should go with them again." Wylie informed Todd.

Barstow said he would take the Carson's Guest Book when he leaves and put it in their cabin after he and the gang cleans up.

"Don't worry, Mrs. Carson, everything is in place," Todd assured his new wife, "we'll just drive around a while so you can digest everything that's happened today. We'll stop by your mom's and pack you a suitcase, and then we will go to our *wedding supper*. As soon as you are comfortable we can go to our cabin."

Kelli was totally amazed at what her new husband had finagled just to marry her, - and how her own mother had been in on the surprise.

As Jake and Angela pulled into the garage, he picked her up and started through the garden and up the stairs. When they got to the top of the stairs, he carried her over the threshold and locked the door behind them.

After a few joyous kisses, he said to her, "I love you my beautiful wife, and now my little kitten, you can be as playful as you want to be."

Being a Ronson

On the way home from the wedding Wiley could see both boys were deep in thought.

Finally, Wayne asked, "Why were you and everybody crying?"

"Because it's a wonderful thing to covenant a genuine relationship with a wife or husband; promising God and your mate your life for as long as you live." Wiley answered.

"You were crying when you had your arm around my mom," Wilson chimed in, "does that mean you want to make this covenant with her?"

"I will not make any covenant with your mother until I can make one with you two boys also." Wiley informed them.

"If you marry us will we be Ronsons too?" Wayne asked.

"I hope so, you wouldn't have to take my name, but I hope you would want to." The big man answered honestly.

"My mom would take your name, huh?" Asked Wilson.

"Yes, son, your mom would take my name." Wiley smiled at Annabelle as he answered.

"But if we don't marry you too, we'd have a different name than my mom?" Wilson continued.

"That's right son, and I'd like for us all to be Ronsons." Wiley responded.

"Why do you always call us son?" Wayne asked.

"I guess I'm daydreaming." Wiley confided.

"You daydream?" Wilson asked.

"Yes, son, I sure do. I've always dreamed and prayed for my

own family and I've daydreamed what it would be like. Now, with you guys, it's better than I dreamed. I think God is answering my prayers big time." The big man had a gleeful sound to his voice, but with a slight quiver, as he answered Wilson.

"Kids always say to us, "Hey Close, stay far, far away from me. I don't want your cooties." They couldn't say that any more, huh?" Wilson continued.

"That's right Wilson, you'd be a Ronson, and no one messes with a Ronson, I'd skin them alive." The big man assured him.

"Does this mean that you would actually adopt us?" Wayne asked Wiley straight up.

"It sure does, with yours and your mother's permissions. We'd be a totally complete family before God and everyone else." Wiley said with joy as he looked over at Annabelle who was smiling so serenely.

She was amazed at how open and honest he was with her boys, and her heart was going Pitter-Pat, Pitter-Pat this time.

"What about a honeymoon, when people gets married they go on a honeymoon, would we have one?" Wayne was still asking the hard questions.

Wiley smiled big as he said, "Absolutely. Your mom and I would go on a honeymoon for a week. Then we'd come back and get you boys and we'd all go on a family honeymoon anywhere you want to go for two weeks."

"Even Disney World?" Wilson asked.

"Absolutely," Wiley assured him, "you two boys will just agree on a place and we'll go."

"Yea, you want to get used to sleeping with Mom before we see you do it." Came Wayne's shocking observation.

"That's right son." Wiley answered matter-of-factly almost swallowing his permanent teeth.

Annabelle's teeth were in danger too as she squeezed Wiley's hand.

"I sure don't want to take you home yet," Wiley was saying, "how about a trip to the City, and finding a nice quiet restaurant for dinner? I think there is one with a bunch of game machines just off of the dining room. It even has a dance floor. Just so we can be together while we are all so good looking."

"Yesss," came two voices from the back seat, "let's go."

Wiley just couldn't leave Annabelle yet, not looking like she does. The excitement of the day was being relived in the back seat as the front seat was throwing sparks and air kisses.

The boys didn't want to order off the menu, they thought that would take too long, they just wanted hamburgers and fries, so that's what Wiley ordered for them. They wanted to get to the game machines. Wiley gave them money to play with.

After inhaling their food, they took off. Wiley and Annabelle were finally alone. There was soft music playing, and the dance floor was empty, it was too early for a crowd. After they ordered their food, Wiley took her hand and led her onto the dance floor. He took her in his big strong arms and held her close as they danced; it felt so good and so right to have her in his arms. His heart could hear her purr. She was beautiful, and she smelled inviting and he could hardly believe what just her touch can do to him.

When he glanced down, she was watching him too, he was sure it was love in her eyes he was seeing as he kissed her softly.

What a mighty God I serve! Was the thought running through his mind.

Todd & Kelli's Wedding Dinner

Todd and Kelli drove around for about an hour talking. They stopped at the *Canyon Casas*, and he showed her where their new home would be when they got it finished.

He had picked her up as soon as she stepped out of the Toyota, partly so her dress wouldn't get dirty, and mostly because he just wanted to hold his new wife close. He kept kissing her over and over, on her lips, her chin and her neck.

"I didn't know you were so romantic; you never said anything about liking me." She whispered to him.

"I didn't want to scare you away until I could figure out a way to make you my wife," he told her as he kissed her again, "I love you so much, I didn't want to take any chances on pushing you away from me."

"I love you too, Todd, and I'm not afraid to go to our cabin after we eat, in fact I'm looking forward to it." She whispered in his ear.

He stood there for quite a while, just cradling his wife in his arms, it was so right and so good.

They headed to Nelli's home. He wanted to fill his wife's mother in on where they would be staying and what the Ranch's phone number is. He also wanted to be sure she had Ira's number.

As the two walked in the door, Nelli had treats for them, a tiny little bridal cake she had made, two glasses of raspberry ice tea, and some mints.

"Just thought I wanted to give you a bit of a reception." Nelli told them as she gave them both hugs.

After talking with Nelli and Walter for a while, Kelli packed herself a bag, and the newlyweds left for their wedding supper.

Ernie had roped off the corner that the big round booth was in and marked it *"reserved."* He had put a big bouquet of fresh red roses on the table. People were starting to filter in but there still weren't too many people in the restaurant. Ernie came over with two menus, and two glasses of Sparkling Cider. He laid the menus down and said he'd be back a bit later.

Todd picked up his glass of Sparkling Cider and handed Kelli's hers as he said, "I toast my lovely wife, the only woman I have ever loved. May we always feel warm and special like we do right now."

He put his arm around her arm and took a sip of his Sparkling Cider, so she did too. They chatted for about fifteen minutes before Ernie came back for their order.

Ernie started the jukebox with soft music, and Todd took his wife's hand and led her onto the dance floor. As he took her into his arms, he could feel her love busting out of her just like his was. She was nuzzling him, and it was all right, she was his wife.

They danced for a while before they went back to the booth, where a beautiful meal with all the fixin's was waiting for them.

As they ate, they were talking about all the things that had happened that day, and what a wondrous day it was. Kelli told her husband how impressed with him she is, and she now believes he can accomplish anything.

Kelli was really surprised about having their own Casa.

"Our very own home, ours, yours and mine, and its brand new," Kelli exclaimed, "and I can walk to work."

"I knew you would like it honey." Todd replied.

When they got ready to leave, Ernie came up to their table. He had put together a breakfast basket that they just needed to pop in the microwave. There were two cups of coffee for each included. Todd thanked him profusely.

As they drove up and parked in front of their little cabin, it looked like it was out of a movie; secluded among the pines, with a little porch. Again, when she stepped out of the Toyota he picked her up and walked to their cabin. The key was in the slot, so Kelli removed it after she unlocked the door. Todd opened the door and carried his little wife over the threshold as he kissed her softly.

He put breakfast in the refrigerator.

Their little Guest Book was on the table; they would look at it later. Right now, his years of dreams were coming true as he kissed his wife.

Annabelle's Tragedy

With lots of lightning and thunder, sadly the basketball practice was rained out again. The teams still had their treats in the back of the amphitheater, so all was not lost.

Wiley asked the boys what they want to pick up for supper, and they both said "Taco Pizzas from *Little Chico's.*"

"You two are going to turn into Pizza Heads." Wiley quipped.

That was all the boys needed to start smart-cracking at each other about pepperoni eyes, mushroom lips, onion eyebrows, pepper teeth and numerous other pizza fixing things. Wiley smiled knowing his boy's imaginations were developing.

The fresh food filled the Jeep with a hunger-making aroma, especially with the windows in to protect them from the rain.

Crrrack, another bolt of awful lightning struck.

"Man, that was close." Wilson remarked.

"Sure was," Wiley responded, "that was a close strike. I could even feel the hair on my arms stand up."

"Me too." Agreed both boys.

Suddenly flames shot up in the dark skies, illuminating the clouds. As Wiley turned down the path to Annabelle's home, he could see that her home had been the target of the terrible lightning, and her trailer was engulfed in the ferocious red flames.

"Oh my God," Wiley exclaimed throwing his cell to Wayne,

"call the sheriff and paramedic Tom Lacey, they're both on the Contact List."

Wiley parked the Jeep back a-ways from the fire as he told the boys, "Stay in the Jeep – no matter what – and start praying hard."

He grabbed the blanket out of the back seat and dipped it in a rain puddle as he took off running. Neighbors were gathering and telling Wiley not to go in the roof was already moving down to crash. He could hear the boys screaming in the background.

Wayne punched Sheriff Leo's button and told him amid cries of agony his mom might be dead, and to call Tom Lacey, the paramedic.

The crying man ran inside the burning trailer with the dampened blanket. He was crawling on his knees as he was screaming, "Annabelle, Annabelle, where are you?"

There was no answer.

As he was feeling around on the floor he felt a small box, it was her cell phone; he stuck it in his pants pocket. Finally, he touched her; she was on the bathroom floor. He didn't know if she was dead or not. Quickly he wrapped the blanket around her as the cracking of demolition was getting louder, and the back-bedroom ceiling caved in.

With brute force he picked her body up with one arm and pulled it up underneath him to shield it from anything falling on it. He could hear more stress creaks. The living room ceiling had now collapsed. He just hoped the kitchen cupboards would hold the roof over them until he could get his lady out of the inferno.

Her legs were dragging behind them as they ran threw his, and other than the light bounces of her body from dragging her across the floor, Annabelle was not moving.

Wiley was praying hard, "God, You gave her to me, protect her now, make her ok. You can't take her away from me now, please God."

The man was in a horror rage. He could hardly get his breath. He could feel things hitting his back.

He could see the door, and as he headed for it he heard

another loud creak as the kitchen ceiling started coming down. He sprang out the door into the air filled with smoke just as the complete ceiling in the kitchen crashed down. His clothes were on fire, and gathering neighbors were dousing him with the rainwater from the puddles.

Annabelle still wasn't moving as he stood up trying to get his equilibrium and run to the Jeep.

He sat her down in the rider's seat as the boys were screaming, "Mommy, Mommy."

They thought she was dead. Wayne was patting down the last bastions of fire from Wiley's shirt as he peeled backward to the road, and then forward toward the church.

"Did you get a hold of Sheriff Leo?" Wiley hollered at Wayne amidst his screams.

"Wayne, did you get a hold of the sheriff?" He asked the boy again.

"Yes, he's calling Mr. Larsen to meet us at the ambulance." Wayne was finally able to answer.

The trip to the paramedic's office was an absolutely horrific trip. No one knew if Annabelle was even alive.

Tom Lacey pulled in right after Wiley, and Alex Caldwell was right behind him. Alex quickly unlocked the office door and then the ambulance rear.

Wiley had Annabelle in his arms running to the vehicle; he knew she needed oxygen immediately. Tom Lacey knew it too and as Wiley lay her down on the gurney he already had the mask on her face and the tank was pumping.

As Alex was shutting the rear door the boys were trying to get in and Alex told them they couldn't go. Wiley hollered at Alex to let his boys in, they must go with their mother. As soon as the boys were in the vehicle, Alex shut the door.

With his remote Alex had opened the big door on the building, jumped in the driver's seat and they were on their way with the siren blazing. Tom was on the telephone to the *Burn Unit* of *City Hospital,* seeking orders for severe burns. The boys were crying so hard that Tom could barely hear the doctor.

Wiley told the boys firmly to quiet down, or Tom couldn't help their mother.

He also told Wayne to call Pastor John; "We need your mother on the prayer chain immediately."

The sobbing young man punched the pastor's name, and Pastor John assured him they would get the prayer chain going immediately, and keep it going until they got some good news.

"Yes, she does have a faint heartbeat, but it's irregular. Her lungs are not working well, and she is in a coma. She was struck by lightning." Tom was telling the burn doctor.

Wiley nodded affirmatively to Tom, he and the boys had seen the crack of lightning, and the trailer was engulfed by the time they turned on her path.

The burn doctor told Tom to get Annabelle's clothes off her fast, and put her in a clean sheet, burns get dangerously infected almost immediately. Tom grabbed clean sheets from the closet. Wiley told the boys to turn around and close their eyes. As Tom and Wiley peeled the fire-destroyed clothes off of her, it was obvious she had very serious burns all over her back. Her front wasn't quite as bad, but as the burned cloth came off the sores started oozing.

"Probably a good thing she is unconscious right now, Wiley," Tom was saying, "this would be horrendous pain if she were awake - these are third degree burns."

It took several minutes to get the clothes peeled out of her burns. Tom said they would lay her on her stomach since the back was so badly damaged. Her hair was burned off the back of her head, and her scalp was weeping.

Wiley laid a clean towel over the back of her head so the boys wouldn't see how bad it looked. After they got Annabelle covered with the clean sheets; Wiley told the boys they could turn back around. She didn't look quite as bad with the clean white sheets.

Tom handed Wiley a hospital gown and told him he should take the burned clothes off his upper torso also, that his wounds were pretty severe too. Both boys started picking the cloth off of Wiley's burns. Wiley could tell they were really grossed out, but they were doing what had to be done; they were becoming Ronsons.

Even amongst the commotion, Wiley was thinking how proud of his boys he is. Tom had given them the sack that contained their mother's clothes to put Wiley's burned frocks in too.

"I'll let the burn doctors clean and put the Silver Sulfadiazine on you, Wiley, they'll be bandaging you too," Tom told him, "with burns being so serious, they need special attention. I can't touch them with anything; just clean what junk out of them I can."

The burn doctor had told Tom to start an IV in Annabelle's arm, and he did, as he kept reporting her vitals to him. She was still breathing, even though it was very shallow. Her heartbeat was very irregular. Annabelle's trailer had taken a heavy bolt, and her survival will only be by the Grace of God.

As Tom finished all the doctor's orders, he stepped back a bit so Wiley could get to Annabelle's head. The big man took her hand and kissed it, then her forehead sticking out from under the towel; he kept praying.

Wayne touched the sheet that was covering his mother's feet, and started praying too, "Please God, please don't let my mom die, please."

His prayers weren't sophisticated, but they were heart prayers, the kind that God hears first. Wiley had told the boys that he firmly believes that God hears a child's prayer first because of their innocence. Wilson was trying to pray too, but was having a hard time. He asked Wiley if God would hear his prayer too since he didn't say the sinner's prayer with Wayne.

Wiley assured him that God would hear his prayer, even though he hadn't said the sinner's prayer.

"Can I say it now?" Wilson asked his big protector.

"Yes, you sure can, son, just repeat after me," Wiley said as he took Wilson's hand and started saying, "Dear Lord Jesus, please forgive all my sins."

"Dear Lord Jesus, please forgive all my sins." Wilson repeated.

Wiley continued, "please come into my heart."

"Please come into my heart." Wilson continued. "And be my Lord and Savior." Wiley added.

"And be my Lord and Savior." Wilson finished.

"Ok, Wilson, you are now a child of God." Wiley told the weeping boy, "You heard what Pastor John said to the seven that were baptized Sunday night, and the same goes for you. Do you accept that charge?"

"I do," Wilson responded, "now if mama dies, I can go to Heaven with her when I die?"

"That's right, son," Wiley assured him, "but I don't think your mother is going to die. God is making us a family, and He's not going to break it up now. You must believe she is going to be all right, that is called faith."

"Now I need to be baptized, Wiley." Wilson urged.

Wiley picked up a bottle of water, and poured some in his hand. He dipped a finger into the puddle of water and rubbed a cross on Wilson's forehead as he said to his boy,

"Wilson Close, I baptize you in the name of the Father, the Son and the Holy Ghost, and into the Lord Jesus Christ."

Then he gave his new Christian son a big hug and roughed up his hair as the young man put his hand on his mother's foot to pray for her too.

Wiley was talking to Annabelle as if she could hear him as they drove, telling her that both of her boys were now ready to meet Jesus if circumstances would deem it.

Tom Lacey was obviously very emotional at what he had just witnessed, and enthralled at this big man's love of the three people he is caring for, and of Jesus Christ.

The special Burn Unit gurney was waiting as Alex pulled into the Emergency Department. There were six nurses and two doctors. They helped Tom pull the ambulance gurney out of the vehicle, and drop the legs. Then rolled the ambulance gurney up beside the hospital gurney, and with the sheets lifted her from one to the other.

Annabelle still didn't move. Wiley thanked Tom and Alex for their help, and said he would be in contact soon.

Both boys were hanging onto Wiley's hands as they walked into the hospital and to the elevator that took them up to the *Burn*

Unit. One burn doctor was perusing Wiley's burns, and ordering a gurney for him.

"I don't need a gurney," Wiley was insisting, "I've got to stay with Annabelle and my boys."

But they ignored his opposition, and a gurney was waiting just outside the elevator door, along with a nurse holding an IV, obviously meant for him.

"I'll lay here as long as you keep my family together," he insisted, "I don't want my boys left alone."

"It's okay, Mr. Ronson," the nurse was telling him, "the boys can stay with you. But, your wife will be going to surgery immediately, and they can't go in the operating room, neither can you."

Wiley didn't bother to correct her when she said "his wife"; it felt kind of good, amidst the pain. The boys each had a hold of one side of his gurney, and they weren't about to turn loose.

Wiley was giving the doctors the details of how the lightning struck her trailer, and it burned quickly, and how she had fire all over her back when he finally found her.

The burn doctor was telling Wiley and the boys, "How they would be debriding her wounds, otherwise known as cleaning them out. They would go with the one-two step fix, which is an artificial skin called Integra. It becomes a good bed for the top layer of grafting. They will be taking a postage sized piece of undamaged skin from both Annabelle and Wiley, and send it to the *Genzyme Tissue Repair Labs* in Massachusetts, where they will grow what is called *Cultured Skin.* This is the best process on the market right now. It will take about three weeks to grow the *Cultured Skin*, and it will be grafted over the *Integra Skin* to form a new top skin layer with minimal scarring. We will have to shave her head completely; all hair must be kept out of her wounds. Her irregular heartbeat, hopefully, will go back to normal when the shock wears off. We will do everything we can to save your mother."

The doctor knew all of the information on grafting wasn't necessary at this moment, but it got the boy's attention, and they were thinking about the process instead of their mother's poor condition.

If the doctors were planning on how to fix her…they must know she will be alright.

The nurses already had the heart monitor on her, and were hooking up a second IV with fluids and antibiotics. First, she asked the boys if they knew of any antibiotics she was allergic to. They didn't. Annabelle would also be given Tetanus and be started on a narcotic for pain and Naproxen for inflammation. The doctor was estimating the surgery to take about six hours.

Wiley jumped off the gurney again, and the two boys kissed Annabelle on her hand, and then Wiley kissed her forehead. As the nurses wheeled her into surgery, the doctor asked Wiley when he received his last *Tetanus*. Wiley told him quite a while ago, so the doctor would be giving him one too, as soon as they could get him back on the gurney.

Wiley told Wayne to get Annabelle's cell out of his pocket and hang on to it. That way they could be in constant contact. As Wayne looked at it, it smelled like smoke, and he took a Kleenex to try and wipe off some of the smell. When he opened it, he pushed the button to check calls. Wiley's name was showing as the last person that she tried to call.

"My mom was trying to call you 'cause she was scared." Wayne told Wiley.

All three men started crying again.

"It's mostly my fault." Wayne announced.

"Oh no, Wayne, why would you say such a thing?" Wiley asked.

"Just 'cause." Wayne replied.

Wiley took Wayne's hand and squeezed it, "No son, it's not your fault at all, just a freak happening of nature."

He could tell Wayne didn't believe him. They would certainly have to discuss this later.

Wiley took out his cell and called Ira, who had heard the news, and right away wanted to know what he could do.

"For one thing," Wiley told him, "I need someone to bring my Jeep down to the hospital, and some clean clothes. I need some extra cash so grab some out of the cash box in the office, Sonny has a key. I need someone who can stay here long enough to take my boys shopping for some clothes; they lost all of theirs in the fire. I also would like for you to check and see if anything is salvageable at the trailer – only if it is safe to go inside. Especially look for Birth or Death Certificates, and Annabelle's Citizenship Certification. If you can't find them, I'll contact Roscoe to get started on replacing them."

Ira readily agreed, he would do everything he could, he knew going inside the trailer would be dangerous, but that's his middle name.

Then Wiley called Sonny, who also knew what had happened, "It's more important now than ever that the home gets finished. It should be there in a few more days, so if you'll be sure they put it where they should, I'd be grateful."

"Don't worry about a thing, Wiley, I'll take care of everything," Sonny assured him, "and how are the boys doing? How is Annabelle? How are you?"

"Annabelle is in bad shape, but we believe that God will give her back to us. The boys are naturally upset. I'm doing fine, just got a few burns." Wiley informed him.

Wiley had barely hung up from talking to Sonny when his phone rang, "This is Wiley."

"Hello Wiley, this is Jess Judd," the voice on the other end exclaimed, "I hate to bring this up right now, but you need to immediately file for temporary custody of the boys, and for *Medical Power of Attorney* over Annabelle. If the *State* finds out she is injured and there are no relatives, they will deem them now indigent and they'll take over custody and care of her and the boys. I know you don't want that."

"Whew," Wiley said as he sighed heavily, "you're right, Jess. I need to keep things in perspective even now. What do I need to do?"

"I'll get with Roscoe tonight and we'll put the papers together and bring them to you to sign early in the morning. We will need the boy's signatures since they are twelve and fourteen. Roscoe and I can take them to a Judge's Chambers right there in the City in the morning. I'll get four-character references and bring them too. I want some with power; John Stoddard will be an excellent reference, along with Mayor Roscoe, Barstow and my dad. Each have stellar records." Jess was informing Wiley.

Jess added, "Mam and Jani are in the Prayer Room, and Emily has the prayer chain going strong. We're all praying for the best."

"Thank you, Jess. If you need a copy of my last Certified Financial Statement from March of this year, I can call Lenore and she'll get it for you." Wiley said thankfully, this could have created a monster, but now, with God's help, he will be able to take care of things.

Just as Wiley hung up his phone rang again. It was Ira. He was sifting through the ashes at the trailer. Ira told Wiley all he found were some cement blocks in the bottom of the bedroom closet. Two flat cap blocks were blocking each side to keep anything from getting into the middle of the two big blocks.

Wiley had turned on the speaker of his cell so he could lay it by his head, and the nurses could still work on his back.

When Wayne heard Ira say he saw cement blocks in the bottom of the closet he hollered into the phone to Ira to bring the can that is hidden in them.

Ira asked Wiley to hold on a moment, and as he lifted up one of the blocks an old metal tennis ball container dropped out onto the closet floor. Ira picked it up and dusted it off as he asked, "What's this?"

"Bring the can to the hospital, it's got important papers in it." Wayne advised.

Ira unscrewed the metal lid, and sure enough, it had papers rolled up in it. Annabelle had stuck it in the middle of the cement blocks for protection, and it had worked. Most of the writing on the old can was melted off, but the can's contents, although a bit scorched, were pretty much intact.

"Wiley," Ira continued as he thumbed through the sheets, "these papers are the kid's *Certified Birth Certificates,* Annabelle's *Citizenship* papers, Wayne Seniors Citizenship papers, and Wayne

Senior's *Certified Death Certificate.* Wow, I'm amazed that Annabelle's little *'safe'* worked."

"Praise God," Wiley shouted, "we'll need all those papers soon. Please bring them with you."

Ira agreed and told Wiley he would check and see if he could find anything else of importance in the morning; it was hard to see anything in the dark with a flashlight.

Wiley asked Ira to stop by the Verizon office and get a charger replacement from Tom Crane for Annabelle's cell and to bring with him. To also have Sonny grab his own charger from his office, that Sonny knows right where it is.

"Please contact Drew Rhein and tell him I need some insurance coverage changes; immediately. He can call me tomorrow." Wiley told Ira.

"I have something very important I need to talk to you both about." Wiley told the two boys after he hung up from talking to Ira, and while he was waiting for the nurses to wheel him into surgery to clean up his wounds. "Since you have no family, if the State finds out your mom is in a coma, they will take you to foster care. I can't let that happen, I don't want you separated from her – or me. Jess and Roscoe are going to draw up papers giving me Temporary Custody of you both, but you'll need to sign the papers. Will you?"

"Yes," both boys agreed, "we don't want to be away from Mama, and we don't want to be away from you neither."

It did Wiley's aching heart good for the boys to say they didn't want to be away from him either.

"Plus, they will take over your mom's care, and we won't have any say in what happens to her. I want her to have the very best care available, so I'm going to take temporary *Power of Attorney* over her health so they can't do anything to her without our permission. Do you understand what I am saying?" Wiley asked them.

"Yes," both boys agreed again, "we don't want no one to say what happens to her but us family."

"Thanks for your trust, boys, we all three want the best for her. Roscoe and Jess will be here tomorrow morning with the papers for us to sign; then they will take them to a Judge. You boys will probably go with them to court, but they will be right with you." Wiley informed the boys.

The nurse came out for the big man's gurney to go into surgery. They had a bunch of papers for Wiley to sign. One of them was for the anesthesia.

"No," Wiley stated flatly, "I do not want to be put to sleep, you can do what you have to, but I intend to remain in control of my faculties in case my family needs me."

"Are you sure, Mr. Ronson?" The nurse asked.

"Absolutely sure," he answered, "just a topical anesthetic will work, and the boys will wait right here until I come out of surgery, is that understood? And please have someone order them a tray of food; they've got to be starved."

"Yes sir." The nurse responded.

The boys were left alone in the surgery waiting room. Their mom in one surgery room, and now their protector in another one. They were frightened, and they were hungry. Their pizza was still in the Jeep back in *Raincroft*.

The boys talked serious talk while they were waiting, and both came to an agreement on what they wanted to do.

Getting His House in Order

About midnight Annabelle was moved to a private room. They had wanted to put Wiley in another room, but he refused, he would stay with Annabelle and the boys. He requested three chairs that the feet come up on to make an almost bed, along with three pillows and blankets. The nurses brought in three matching lounge chairs. With Wylie's rolling IV stand he could pretty much move around freely.

    The boys had had some supper, and were so tired they agreed to sit down in the chairs and relax. Both said they would be staying awake with Wiley. Wasn't long before both had fallen asleep, so Wiley covered them up with the nice warm sheet-blankets the nurse had brought in. His lady was still lying silently on her tummy. The oxygen, heart monitor, vital signs machine and IV's were still running. They had an aspirator hooked up trying to pull the gunk out of her lungs. She was a maze of bandages.

    Wiley checked her feet. She had shoes on when she was struck, and the shoes had prevented some of the fire from burning the bottom of her feet too badly or scraping them up while he was dragging her out of the burning home. Her head was bandaged with the same gauze that covered most of her body. He really felt he could see her taking a-bit deeper breaths, but she still hadn't moved. Wiley took her hand and started praying again.

    He started softly calling to her, "Come back Annabelle, come back to us. We need you Annabelle. The boys and I love you so much, please come back to us."

    "Please God, give her some of my strength through my touch.

Please Jesus, flow some strength into her. I cover her with Your Precious Blood Lord, I claim her healing in Your Name." Wiley was sobbing as he prayed.

He had heard that even a person in a coma can hear, and he was determined to keep talking to her.

About two in the morning, he became so tired he laid his head down on the side of her bed. He wanted to lightly doze, hopefully enough to get some rest, but awake enough he could keep track of what was going on as the nurses came in every few moments and checked his wounded little lady.

He was still holding her hand when he woke up at five o'clock with his own pain racking his body. He could hear the food cart being rolled down the hallway. He checked his little lady, but she hadn't moved. He started praying again, between times of telling her that he and the boys love her and she must come back to them. He was also praying that he might be able to withstand the pain he was having so he wouldn't have to take any pain medication that would cloud his judgment. He did agree, however, to take some Aleve. The nurse brought him three Aleve, with his size and amount of pain three were called for.

By seven the boys were waking up and wanting to know how their mother was doing.

"She's holding her own, sons," he told them, "we just have to love her back to us."

"I heard you tell her you love her more'n once." Wayne piped up.

"Yes, I did, because I do," Wiley answered, "your mother is the love of my life, the only woman I have ever loved."

"She might be ugly now, Wiley, but you said you wanted a family so bad that you would even take an ugly wife." Wilson chimed in.

Wiley about split a gut trying not to laugh. Even in misery there can be humor. He thought to himself.

"Wilson, I don't care what your mother looks like, she will never be ugly, and I will always love her." Wiley informed him.

"You saw her without clothes; doesn't that mean you have to

marry her now?" Wilson piped up.

"What if she does die, Wiley, do you still want to adopt us?" Wayne asked another one of his pointed questions.

"I sure do," Wiley guaranteed him, "but your mom is not going to die, we will love her back to health. Just keep telling your mother that you love her, and to please come back to you. We have to exercise faith now boys, just keep praying."

Jess and Roscoe were there by nine o'clock with the papers. Wiley read as much as he could, so did Wayne.

"Gimme a pen," Wayne said, "we both want to sign them right now."

Jess handed Wayne a pen, and after he signed he handed the pen to Wilson, who signed too.

Wiley was busy signing his papers as he said to Jess, "I'm thinking it might be a good idea for my boys to go with you to verify their signatures."

"Good idea, it might come in handy to have them with us. Then we'll get them a good meal before we bring them back." Jess affirmed.

The boys each gave Wiley a very easy hug before they left.

Jess was almost crying, he had a wonderful father, and now these two little boys will also.

When the four got to the courthouse, the boys were overwhelmed with how big it was, and how fancy. Roscoe asked to be assigned a Judge, and they were given *Family Court Judge Roy Barton.* Roscoe knew Judge Barton to be a fair and honest judge, and he was really glad for this Assignment.

They didn't sit long before the judge's court reporter came out to get them saying; "Judge Barton will see you in his Chambers. This way please."

"We don't get to stand up in front of the judges' big desk?" Wilson asked.

"Not today." The reporter answered.

When they walked into the judge's Chambers the boys didn't have the slightest idea of how to greet a judge, so they bowed to him several times. Jess caught the Judges twinkling eyes as he looked down trying not to laugh.

"Please sit down." The judge told them.

"We want Wiley to be in charge of us." Wayne spoke up without waiting for Jess to give the judge the papers.

"I see," the judge responded, "and who is Wiley?"

"He's the man that my mom and us boys are going to marry and get adopted to."

"I see," the judge replied, "you love Wiley and you're going to get married?"

"Yes sir." Wayne said matter-of-factly.

"We ain't told him yes yet," Wilson chimed in, "he asked us a long time ago but we haven't said yes yet. But we're going to this afternoon. Then when our mom wakes up she'll be happy 'cause she loves Wiley too."

"Very interesting," Judge Barton said, "you love this Wiley? And you're going to marry him?"

"That's right, Mr. Judge," Wayne came back, "and we're all going to go on a honeymoon for two weeks after Wiley and mom goes on one for a week first. That's so they'll get used to sleeping with each other before we're around."

The judge was now covering his mouth, but Jess and Roscoe could see the smile lines peeking from behind his hand, and the creases in the corner of his eyes.

"Yea," Wilson chimed in, "Wiley's rich and bought us a new home, and we get to decide where to go on our honeymoon."

"I see," said the Judge again, "and where are you boys planning on going for your honeymoon?"

"Probably Disney World in Florida, cause we both like that place." Wilson answered, "Wiley always said he wanted a family, and he'd even take an ugly wife. My mom was really pretty, but she's all burned now, so he might get his ugly wife."

"My mom is really bad, and if she dies, Wiley is gonna adopt us anyway. He says we are his boys from God." Wayne spoke up.

The Judge looked at Roscoe; "you are Mayor Martin from *Raincroft* aren't you?"

"That I am." Roscoe responded.

"You are vouching for the man Wiley?" Judge Barton asked.

"I certainly am, known him all his life, good man, honest and well healed." Roscoe replied.

"You been looking at Wiley's heels?" Wilson asked Roscoe.

"No, that's just a saying." Roscoe responded.

"Thas a funny one." Wilson reasoned.

Suddenly Wilson started telling the judge how Wiley went into the burning trailer after his mom got struck by lightning. How his clothes were on fire too, and they helped put him out. How the paramedics were not going to let them go with their mom to the hospital, but Wiley said they would be going, they need to be with their mom. The judge listened patiently.

"Let me see the paperwork." Judge Barton requested.

Jess lay the open file down in front of the judge. He perused the papers for only a moment, then said, "It is so ordered."

The judge signed all of the papers for both requests, then held his hand out to shake with the boys.

"Wow," Wilson said, "I get to shake hands with a real judge. Wait til I tell Wiley. He'll be impressed."

"I'd like to meet this Wiley," the judge remarked as he handed the papers back to Jess, "thank you for a very pleasant case."

Wayne was mulling over *pleasant case* as they walked out of the courthouse. He wasn't sure what the judge meant.

Jess asked the boys where they wanted to eat, and a unanimous answer came, *"The Sweet Dragon."*

When they stepped back into Annabelle's room, Wiley was still sitting holding her hand.

"We didn't have to say a word; the boys presented their own cases. You've got both Legal Custody of the boys and Power of Attorney for Annabelle." Jess told Wiley.

The big man let go of Annabelle's hand long enough to give his boys hugs through his tears.

"Now, Jess and Mr. Martin, you be our witnesses." Wayne said as he took one of Wiley's hands and Wilson took the other.

They each dropped down on one knee as they said together,

"Wiley Ronson, we've decided we'll marry you, so will you marry us?"

There was not a dry eye in the place, not even the two nurses that were watching the proceedings.

"Wow, yes, yes, yes." The big man exclaimed as he grabbed both of his sons and gave them as close to a bear hug as his Frankenstein arms would allow, and carried them over near their mother's head so they could tell her they are all going to be a family.

Jess and Roscoe stopped by the hospital office and gave the secretary a copy of the Power of Attorney for Annabelle.

On the way home Jess and Roscoe were remarking that it's no wonder Wiley loves those boys so much, they are really something. Jess could hardly wait to tell Mam. She will be delighted.

About one o'clock, Ira and Sonny showed up. They had brought clean clothes for Wiley, but were both wondering how he was going to get them on over all the bandages. Before Ira or Sonny could get a complete sentence out of their mouths the boys were telling them that they were all getting married as soon as their mom wakes up.

"Probably right here in the hospital." Wayne spoke up.

Ira handed Wiley the old tube with the important papers, Wiley's cell charger and a new one for Annabelle's phone.

Wiley was grinning ear to ear, so they knew it was true.

"I understand we need to do some clothes shopping for your boys." Ira stated.

"Sure do," Wayne chimed in, "our Dad wants us to be dressed good, we're going to be Ronsons."

Wiley handed Ira back some of the cash he had brought, and the four guys took off to do some serious shopping – and probably eat at a place with machines.

"Annabelle, honey, can you hear me? The boys are excited about us getting married. I love you Annabelle, I hope you can hear me. Please come back to us, we want you, and love you so much. Please come back." Wiley said softly to his little wounded lady as he kissed her forehead, and then her hands.

Something in his heart was telling him she is a bit better, she will live. He sat back down and took her hand again and started praying and talking to her softly.

The doctors came in to check her wounds, they were very raw, but so far, no infection. He checked Wiley's also and his had no sign of infection either.

When the boys got back he would figure out how to take a shower and get some of the smoke off of him, and would just pitch the shoes and pants.

As he sat there watching her breathe, he thanked God that He had spared his lady. He thought her breathing seemed just a bit more pronounced; she didn't seem to be gasping so much. *Wayne wants to get married as soon as she wakes up; he was thinking to himself, my insurance is top of the line, with no pre-existing conditions clauses. The minute we get married my insurance will cover Annabelle and the boys. Roscoe said the adoption would just be a matter of a few papers to sign, a criminal background check, and about a ten-month waiting period. Hmmm, I wonder, since I've got legal custody now – perhaps the boys are covered now, I'll have to talk to Drew Rhein tomorrow and check on my insurance.*

Her recuperating time will be long, I'm anticipating, and I will be able to be with her since we will be married. I think Wayne probably has a very good idea. We'll talk about it. Got to teach Wayne to drive, he's almost fifteen, and can get a Learner's Permit. He can shop and run errands. Maybe I need to get him a golf cart like Angela's. The big man's mind was going rampant with ideas.

The boys jumped back into the room; really excited as they lay the clothes out over the lounge chairs for Wiley to see.

"Good job," he told them as he looked at every single piece, "extra shoes too, you've thought of everything."

The boys were trying to find hangers to hang their new clothes in the closet and ended up asking the nurse for more hangars.

Wiley thanked his friends for bringing the Jeep, phone chargers, and especially the old metal tube…and for taking his boys shopping. The shopping trip was therapy for his boys.

Ira told him he was going back to *Raincroft* now so he could go through the trailer again before dark. Ira handed Wiley the Jeep key; everyone said their good-byes and the two mountain men left.

As they pulled into *Raincroft*, and passed by Annabelle's lot, there were two semi tractors sitting in front, each with half a home hitched on the back.

They are several days early." Sonny remarked to Ira as he jumped out of the black truck.

Wiley was sitting patiently by Annabelle's side, holding her hand and praying, and the boys were snoozing in their chairs. Wiley's ringing phone startled him back to reality.

It was Sonny; "The home is here. The extra truck got back early so they decided to bring it now, and are putting it on the lot as we speak. I've told them exactly how it is to be."

"WOW, praise the Lord," Wiley exclaimed so loudly it woke up the two boys, "thanks for taking care of the setting up. God knew we'd need it sooner."

"Boys, did you hear that? Your new home has arrived and Sonny is telling the drivers how to set it up at this very moment." Wiley related to them.

They started jumping around with glee. Soon Wiley had joined them. It was such a blessing to have something good happen after the past couple of days.

Apparently, their glee had gotten through to Annabelle, because she raised her thumb into the air.

"Praise God, Praise God." The big man said as he touched the thumb that his wounded lady was holding up.

It relaxed back down as the boys watched with Wiley. This was a very encouraging sign. She would be coming back to them, she had moved, she is alive.

Wiley just kept kissing her hand and then her forehead and telling her how much he and the boys love her. It was all right now to speak his love of her out loud.

Later Wiley asked Wayne to please sit down; he wanted to talk to him. Wayne sat down in the chair right beside of Wiley's as the big man started talking, "Son, why in the world would you think you have any responsibility in your mom's accident?"

The young man just sat quietly as his eyes filled up with tears.

"Please tell me, son, it's ok, everything is going to be all right." Wiley was encouraging him to talk to him.

It took several minutes of the two just sitting looking at each other before Wayne finally spoke, "My mom wouldn't been 'lectrocuted if I hadn't waited so long to say I'd marry you. Then she wouldn't have been alone."

"Oh, my goodness, Wayne, that's so not true, she would probably have been alone anyway, her new home hadn't gotten here yet." Wiley responded.

"Yea, but if you were married, she'd of been at your house." Wayne insisted.

"No, son, my little apartment in my shop is only an efficiency, and wouldn't hold our family." Wiley assured him as he put his arms around him.

"But, you would probably have put us all in an apartment or at the motel, instead of staying there." Wayne insisted.

"No, Wayne, we would have stayed there as a family until our new home was delivered. Absolutely none of your mother's injuries are in any way your fault. As a family we will get through this ordeal, have faith, my son, God will make everything right. We will all be all right." Wiley repeated his assurance.

"Me too," Wilson added, "I helped Wayne not answer you."

Wiley put his arm around Wilson too as he said, "No, my other son, there is no way you or your brother had any part in your mom's accident. It was just an accident, it wasn't planned, it just happened. It was a freak of nature, and it was no one's fault."

The Waiting

Two more days passed before Annabelle moved again. Wiley had sat there the entire time. The boys had gotten to know the whole hospital, especially the cafeteria. They were bringing Wiley up lunches they would like. He ate them without a word of complaint, even though they were bringing him soda – which he rarely drank before. He had lots of French fries, and hamburgers with lots of ketchup - but without onions.

Wiley was dipping a fry in ketchup when Annabelle moved again. He jumped to his feet and punched the nurse's button. As he looked excitedly at her, she tried to open her eyes.

Joy filled his heart, as he called the boys to look also; "Your mom's waking up, your mom's waking up."

As the boys jumped to their feet, they got to see her before she shut her eyes again. Praise the Lord, she was waking up, and all the prayers were working.

"Annabelle my love. You're going to be all right Honey. You're going to be all right. The boys are here and they are all right too." Wiley was saying to her as she drifted back off – this time it was more of a sleep status than a coma.

He was sure she had heard him, and hoped she would find comfort in his words. Her heart monitor was now a lot more stable, and her lungs were functioning much better, so the aspiration tube had been taken out. Now he could see her beautiful lips, she would be able to smile.

The boys were depressed that she had drifted off, but Wiley told them she was sleeping this time, not in a coma, and that the strong medicines they were giving her would keep her sleepy. That seemed to satisfy them, it was good to have Wiley with them, and he always knew what was going on.

Wiley was exhausted; you could see it on his face. He had been up for days with almost no sleep.

About ten o'clock in the morning, a huge surprise walked in. It was Jake and Angela. They had heard the news and cut their honeymoon short. Wiley couldn't believe it as he gave Jake a big hug. The two men just held each other for several minutes. They had been great friends since childhood, and had always been able to feel each other's hurts. Jake could certainly feel his friends hurt, and his exhaustion, along with the pain that was radiating under the bandages on his back.

"This is my dad's best friend," Wayne said to the nurse that had come in to check Annabelle.

Jake asked her to bring in a gurney; Wiley was going to get some sleep.

"I can't sleep, Jake." Wiley informed him.

"Oh yes you can, my friend, my wife and I will stay as long as necessary. Now we can either do this the easy way, or the hard way, and I'm in a lot better shape than you right now Wiley Ronson." Jake reminded him.

"You cut your honeymoon short just to come?" Wiley asked amid tears of joy.

"Absolutely, we'll be married forever, and we have lots of time to honeymoon." Jake affirmed, as he almost pushed his big friend over to the gurney and down onto his stomach.

The nurse had barely put the sheet over Wiley before he was sound asleep. It's so good to have friends you can trust.

Jake asked the boys to very quietly tell him everything, starting from the rained-out basketball practice. They were so excited to be telling Jake the story, and they told him everything. Wilson even told how Wiley had seen their mom naked in the ambulance so now he had to marry her. Their eyes were as big as dollars as they talked. They told him how they even shook hands with a judge, and that they were all going to be married now, and they were going to be Ronsons because Wiley was adopting them.

Wilson also piped up about how Wiley had told God he would take an ugly wife because he wanted one so badly, and he's getting one now.

"Your mother will never be ugly to Wiley," Jake assured Wilson, "she will always be beautiful in his eyes because he loves her so much. Just like I love my beautiful wife Angela."

Angela was talking to Annabelle, telling her they would be staying with her family for a while, that she was going to be all right, and that Wiley was finally sleeping. She had taken Annabelle's hand, and thought she could feel a slight squeeze. She told Jake, and he came over to talk to Annabelle, and as he took her hand, he felt the slight squeeze also. Then it was the boy's turn to feel life in their mother. They became ecstatic and Jake had to keep putting his finger over his lips to tell them to be very quiet.

"I think I'll take the boys down to the cafeteria for a while, Mrs. Judd, if you'll stay here with Annabelle." Jake said to his sweetheart.

"Sure will, Mr. Judd." His lovely wife responded as they kissed good bye. Jake thought he needed to keep the boys out of the room so their dad could sleep.

The boys were a bit stir-crazy too, so Jake walked around the hospital grounds after they had eaten. He showed them his big bike, and they immediately fell in love. He took the boys for a ride around the parking lot, one in the sidecar, and one on the saddle. The tragedy they had been through seemed to be a bit dim in their glee of riding the big bike. Jake couldn't take them out of the parking lot because he didn't have a third helmet and certainly wouldn't put them in danger. The boys felt 'big' wearing the helmets even around the parking lot.

"As soon as my mom wakes up, we're gonna have the wedding right here in the hospital." Wayne was saying as they walked back into the building.

"Does your dad know about getting married right here in the hospital?" Jake asked.

"We mentioned it, but he's been so upset I don't know if he remembers," Wayne answered, "so will you stay and stand up with us?"

"Yes, we will, boys," Jake informed him, "but there's a lot of planning to do for a wedding."

"All we need is a *Gift Certificate,* and some rings," Wilson chimed in, "and we can get a bouquet down in the gift shop. We've been looking there and we think we've found the one we want, and it's not too 'spensive."

"As soon as we're married, my mom will have Wiley's insurance 'cause there's no waiting period," Wayne added, "and maybe since you're here we can go with our new dad and pick out the rings."

"Yea," Wilson chimed in again, "then all we need is a veil for her face, that'll cover her sores."

"Sonny said our new home was delivered day before yesterday, and he is making sure it's all set up right," Wayne injected, "so when we take mom to our new home it will be okay for Wiley to stay with us 'caus we'll be married."

Jake was impressed at how the boys were planning the wedding, and their future lives. Wilson is such a hoot that Jake was having trouble keeping a straight face as he thought to himself, *Children sure have a way of cutting through situations with straight up honesty. It's sometimes comical how a child hears something in a different format than what was originally said.*

Jake was now up to full steam, even to Wilson's accepting Christ and being baptized in the ambulance. Jake was thrilled that these two remarkable boys would soon be his Godchildren, and just like their new father, he would take their lives very seriously.

Wedding Plans Continue

Wiley slept about seven hours before he woke up to his boys checking on him. As he opened his eyes he could see two sets of eyes peering back at him. His heart filled with joy; they were worried about his sleeping so long. He was always up and going, and had things under control. Now, sleeping, he was at everyone's mercy, and the boys didn't like that feeling. However, the boys knew that Jake was there, so everything was actually all right.

Their excitement seemed to be getting the best of them. They were making up lists for the wedding plans; including jewelry, clothing – and - of course, treats.

"Hi, my sons, "Wiley said to them, "how long have I been asleep?"

"Seven hours, "Wayne answered, "but Jake's here."

"We need to get the wedding plans fixed," Wilson commented, "how do we get our *Gift Certificate?* Besides, we men need our wedding rings too."

"It's a *Marriage Certificate*, Wilson." His brother cut in.

"Whatever." Wilson resolved.

"The law says your mother has to sign and show proof of who she is to get a *Marriage License*," Wiley advised them, "and right now there is no way she can make it to the County Clerk's Office to apply for one."

"But there must be some way to get it." Wayne insisted.

Wiley could see the wheels turning in Wayne's head as he got up off the gurney and headed over to check on his wounded lady.

"She's moved a couple mor' times." Angela informed Wiley.

"Annabelle, Baby, can you hear me? Please squeeze my hand." Wiley whispered in her ear.

To his delight, he could feel her slightly squeeze his hand as she responded to his voice and touch.

"Can you smile Sweetie?" He anxiously asked her as he watched her lips.

There it was – a small smile. She was aware of him. Wiley was overwhelmed with gratefulness as he leaned over and gently kissed her smiling lips.

"I love you Annabelle Close, and we are going to be a family. The boys have given us their blessings," he told her with his heart still filled with joy, "will you marry me?"

She didn't answer: she had fallen asleep again.

"The boys have been busy for hours planning their wedding. They are expecting wedding rings for them as well as their mother, and I think they are planning on shopping for new wedding clothes." Jake informed his big friend.

Amid chuckles Wiley responded, "Having a couple of sons is a hoot, and I'm not about to dash their plans for their own wedding rings. In fact, it sounds like a good idea to me!"

When Jake and Angela took the boys down to the cafeteria for lunch, Jake couldn't help but notice that Wayne was still deep in thought, so he asked him, "What are you thinking so hard about, Wayne? You're going to drain your brain."

"Wiley said my mom has to go to sign for the Marriage License and prove who she is. But she can't. It might be a long time before she can leave the hospital. Must be something can be done." Wayne said thoughtfully

As Jake watched his young friend speak, an idea started running through his mind, so he said to the boys, "I don't know if it can work or not, but if we somehow could do an *Affidavit of Identity* and get *Power of Attorney* from Annabelle by a non-connected third party with some clout for signing for her to get the Marriage License, that might be a way of getting around her appearing at the County Clerk's Office."

Wayne listened intently, hanging on every word Jake was saying. Wilson was watching and listening too but didn't seem to understand what his soon to be Godfather was saying. Wayne didn't reply to Jake, but the wheels were obviously turning: Jake could almost hear them grinding.

Wiley was sitting by Annabelle holding her hand, reading the Bible to her and praying when she moved again. He looked up, and she was looking at him.

"Annabelle Baby," he said with joy, "you're awake. Can you speak?"

"I-I thin' so," came her welcome words, "how ar' the boys?"

"They are fine, Honey, they are down in the cafeteria with Jake and Angela." He told her amid tears of joy.

"Jake and Angela are here?" She asked.

"Yes, Baby, they cut their honeymoon short to be with us," Wiley informed her, "and they will be here as long as necessary. They will stand up with us when we get married. Did you hear me ask you to be my wife?"

"Yes, I remember, but I tho't I's dreamin', Wiley," Annabelle answered, "but ya don' really wan' ta marry me lookin' like this, yu deserve someone much better."

"There is no one better for me, Annabelle, than you! You are the only woman I have ever loved – or wanted. Our boys want us to be a family too; they have given us their blessings. Please say you'll be my wife, you'll make everything I've dreamed of, but thought I could never have, come true. Plus, I'll have two sons to carry on my name because they want me to adopt them. Please, my beautiful Annabelle, say you will marry me." Wiley pleaded.

"Yur not askin' me out o' pity, Wiley?" She inquired.

"No Baby, only out of love for you and my boys." He assured her.

"Well, if yur sure, yes Wiley Ronson, I will marry you." She agreed.

He moved his lips to hers and kissed her softly and gently, and as she kissed him back he said, "Your lips still work great, Baby. Annabelle, I honestly love you, and I love our boys too."

The *'our boys'* got deep within her heart; her sons were not excess baggage, they were wanted too by this wonderful man. They would be a real family. She puckered her lips for another kiss, and Wiley sure was ready.

"Pleas' 'ave the doctor's stop som' of the medicines tha' keeps me asleep, the pain ain't so bad now. I want to wake up." Wiley's wounded lady asked him.

"Okay Baby, if you are sure you don't need the knock out meds, I will ask them to back off on some of the drugs. But, you must promise to tell me if you start hurting badly again. I don't want you in a lot of pain, okay?" He reasoned with her.

"I Promise." Annabelle agreed as she drifted back off to sleep.

Wiley sat there for several minutes weeping softly. They were tears of joy and thanksgiving to The Lord for bringing her back to him, and for giving him this beautiful lady to be his wife. And for giving him two heirs, two especially fine boys.

When he could speak again, he pushed the button for the nurse. She came in and he told her what Annabelle had said. The nurse said she would call the doctor for new PRN orders. As the nurse was leaving, Jake, Angela and the boys came into the room. It was obvious Wiley was emotional and had been weeping.

"What's wrong?" Wayne asked with concern.

"Nothing, son, not a thing," Wiley related, "in fact everything is great. Your mother woke up and was talking to me. She has agreed to be my wife, and wants the drugs putting her to sleep all the time reduced so she can wake up and talk with us."

As Wiley hugged his boys Wayne spoke up, "We need to go get the rings and our wedding suits."

"Yea," exclaimed Wilson, "and we want to go to NewMan Marbles so we can get the same suits we had like yours that got all burned up."

"It's not *NewMan Marbles*," Wayne scolded, "it's Neiman Marcus"

"Whatever." Wilson shrugged.

Wiley looked at Jake, and the two men started laughing.

"My wife and I will be here, so you guys go do what you need to do to get ready for your weddings." Jake assured his friend.

Both boys beat Wiley to his Jeep, and had their seat belts fastened by the time Wiley got the driver's door open. Boys tend to make noises when they are excited: and all sorts of funny sounds were coming from the back seat; from giggles to shrieks. Wayne and Wilson were totally stoked about their mom waking up and talking – and about the excitement of planning a wedding themselves – immediately.

The boys wanted to go first to *The Jewelry Palace*.

Wiley pulled in to the parking lot and the boys bounced into the store like they were on pogo sticks. Headed directly to the men's rings, Wayne requested the salesman to bring the ring case out of the showcase, but he seemed hesitant. But as Wiley nodded his approval, the case was set on the counter, and the boys looked at each one.

"You look like you've been through a storm." The salesman remarked to Wiley as he perused all of his bandages.

"A lightning storm," the bandaged man tended, "I doubt that Frankenstein ever drove a vehicle."

Most of the rings were much too big for them as they tried every one on their left ring fingers.

"Here," Wiley told them, "let's try them on the big finger of your right hand. See, your left ring finger is for your wife's wedding ring only. Our wedding rings will be on your right hands. We'll get ones to fit your large middle fingers so as your fingers get bigger, you will be able to transfer the ring to your right ring finger, and it should fit for a long time. And, if it gets too small, we can have it re-sized to fit."

Then the boys had to try each and every ring on their right middle fingers.

All the rings were still too large, and Wiley saw their dilemma as he assured them, "The rings will be sized to fit you perfectly. After you pick out the ring you like the salesman will measure all three of our fingers so they can be sized correctly."

"You're getting a ring to match ours?" Wilson asked.

"Sure am," Wiley answered ruffling Wilson's hair, "we three Ronson guys will match."

Both boys loved that remark.

The young men settled on a gold band that had a star in the center top of it, with a diamond in it.

"Wow," Wilson exclaimed, "we'll have a real diamond. Now the kids won't make fun of us any more for being so poor."

Wiley's heart ached for the bullying his boys had suffered all their young lives. *Never again!* The big man's mind determined.

"I guess we'll take these, if it's ok with our dad." Wayne informed the salesman as Wiley nodded his approval.

"I want the boy's names engraved on the inside of their rings. One is Wayne Ronson, and the other is Wilson Ronson." Wiley told the salesman.

"And my dad's will say Wiley Ronson." Wilson proclaimed.

Their fingers were measured and each name was written on a piece of paper to accompany each ring to the engraver, as Wilson asked the salesman, "Do we get the pretty boxes to put them in too?"

"Sure do." The salesman agreed.

"But our dad needs a chain to put my mom's rings around his neck like Jake did." Wilson exclaimed.

"Jake? A rather large bearded mountain man, with a little red head?" The salesman asked Wiley.

"Yep, Jake is going to be my boys' Godfather." Wiley announced.

The salesman smiled.

Next – to the women's rings. Of course, the boys wanted to look at all of them. But as the salesman unlocked the display case, the boys had already focused on one set with a heart diamond in the center.

"I like that one." Wayne remarked.

"Me too," Wilson chimed in, but that's lots of money!"

Along with the heart center diamond, the engagement ring had two heart diamonds on each side. The wedding band had five heart diamonds lined up in it. It was 'bent' to fit around the big heart in the engagement ring.

"You know, boys, I think that's my favorite too," Wiley agreed with his sons, "I think those are our choice."

Wiley tried the rings on his little finger, as the boys tried them on their ring fingers too. They were snug and wouldn't go all the way on, so Wiley figured they would fit Annabelle's finger. If they didn't fit now she could come into the store herself when she was better and they could be sized then. However, Wiley felt they probably would fit because he had felt her fingers often as he held her hands. The three gave their unanimous approval.

While Wiley and the salesman were finishing writing up the orders on the rings, Wilson had run over to the neck chain department and had already picked out one for his dad to put the rings on around his neck like Jake did. They would be taking Annabelle's set today, but they would have to come back tomorrow to get the men's rings.

"We still want the velvet boxes even though my dad will have the rings around his neck." Wilson informed the salesman, apparently wanting to get their money's worth.

The big man was realizing more and more where each of his boy's talents lay.

The salesman handed the sack to Wiley after his bank cleared the check; Wayne put his hand out for the package. Wiley handed it to him, and Wayne opened the velvet box and took the chain out of it. Then he opened the velvet box that had Annabelle's rings in it and carefully took them out and put them on the chain. He held the chain up to Wiley, who bent over so his son could put the chain on his neck. The happy man could tell that the boys took this as an official act of confirmation and approval of his engagement and marriage to their mom.

How many parents miss this kind of imagination and special moments by rushing their kids? The wonderful big man thought to himself.

Lasting Moments Floral Boutique was right next door to the jewelry store. Wilson asked if they could go in a look at flowers, and Wiley agreed.

"If we get her silk flowers, they will last forever and she can take them home and decorate our new home." Wilson told Wiley – who was grinning from ear to ear; having two sons is a blast. Even better than he had dreamed.

Naomi Pratt greeted them as they walked in. She had opened the shop about five years ago, and it was doing very well.

There was a beautiful bouquet with white roses and blue carnations, along with baby's breath and vines cascading about eighteen inches.

"Can we get this one?" Wayne asked, "I think blue and white are perfect colors for our wedding."

"Absolutely, it's perfect." Wiley agreed.

"Now we need five blue flowers to match these ones in mom's flowers," Wayne continued as he pointed to the blue carnations, "one for each of us and one for Jake and for Pastor John Stoddard. And, we need two flowers for Angela's bouquet to match my mom's."

"Don't forget Todd's and Barstow's carnations. Also, Kelli's, Mia's and Emily's corsages', with a blue carnation and a white rose." Wilson added.

"Oh yea, and we shouldn't forget Jani, she will be helping Mom dress. And we don't want to forget Sonny, Ira and Billy are helping with treats. Besides Ira is almost family because he's Jake's blood brother now. And Jess helped with the Legal work, and Beth will be with Jess, so she shouldn't be the only one without a flower." Wayne added.

"And, of course, Deputy Homer shouldn't be left out 'cause he's almost family and as soon as he marries Jani he will be. The Judge certainly needs one 'cause he helped us do this." Wilson exclaimed.

"Right!" Wayne agreed.

Wiley's amusement was so evitable as he watched his sons calculating and planning the big event. *Looks like everyone at the ceremony will be decorated. Nothing gets by my boys; they've even noticed the sparks between Homer and Jani.*

"Okay, we're ready to order." Wayne announced.

"Yea, we'll need 11 boutonnieres of one blue carnation. We only need 10, but in case we forgot someone, we need to be prepared." Wilson ordered.

"Then for the women folk, we need my mom's – that one in the case, and a bouquet for Angela with two blue carnations and some little white roses and that baby's breath stuff. Please put white satin ribbon og will match." Wayne proposed.

"We'll need 5 girl's flowers, made up with one blue carnation, and two baby roses and a bow for Kelli, Emily, Mia, Jani and Beth." Wilson added to his order.

"And don't forget the white ribbon, but it has to be smaller 'cause their flowers are smaller than my mom's, and we need them tonight or early in the morning." Wayne added.

Wiley was almost in stitches inside as he watched these industrious young men preparing a very formal ceremony. He noticed Naomi's enduring smile too.

"Well," Naomi remarked as she was finishing up the order, "I have the boutonnieres already, and, of course, the cascade in the showcase is ready to go, so all I have to make are the five ladies' corsages. I think I can have them ready in about 3 hours. My helper is in the back now, and I'll put her right on it. The silk flowers are already made in stock, so it's just a matter of putting them together."

"And adding the ribbon." Wilson included.

She nodded as she smiled.

Wilson thought they probably needed to eat...

"After we get our wedding clothes." Wayne advised.

As the big man settled up the bill he was thinking, Yep, my boys do have hollow legs.

As the trio walked into Neiman Marcus to look at suits, the boys were reminding Wiley that they wanted the same kind of suits as they had for Jake and Angela's wedding that had burned up in the fire. The big man chuckled to himself remembering that Wilson had called the store "NoMan Marbles".

With Wiley's still having bandages all over his back, he could just drape his suit jacket over his shoulders. An XXXL shirt should go over the bandages. He would have Sonny bring him his suit from Jake's wedding.

The boys were really delighted when they found the exact suits and accessories; Wiley noticed tears in Wayne's eyes. He felt deeply for the losses the boys had suffered, not because they had anything expensive, but because they had lost all their little trinkets that meant something personal to them; along with their school work and even notes from their dad.

Wiley remembered the two little notes he still has from his own dad, and remorse hit down deep in him as he imagined how he would feel to lose the little pieces of paper. He put his arm around Wayne and hugged him as he whispered that he was sorry for his great loss.

The big man knew that there would probably be many flashbacks; and he asked God to let him be cognizant of when they happen, and give him the words to comfort his sons.

After all the clothes and shoes were purchased, the boys headed for the men's cologne counter; "real men must smell good," they were chanting.

The nurse changed the bandages and cleaned Wiley's wounds that morning, and she had put even smaller bandages on him. He could bend his arms now; they weren't stretched out like Frankenstein's. In a few hours he would be able to put them around his new wife.

When the nurse changed and debrided Annabelle's wounds that morning, she also cut down the size of her bandages, and still no infection was obvious. She too could bend her arms better.

With the burns healing so nicely, soon the doctors could start the grafting process on both of them. That was blessed good news. Wiley hoped he would be able to take his family home for a few days, and then come back for the skin grafting surgery. He knew; however, he would have to wait until Annabelle was mobile and roadworthy.

As they ate Wiley ask Wayne what made him so sure Pastor John Stoddard would drive all the way to the City to marry them.

"Just 'cause I'm going to ask him in faith." Wayne stated matter-of-factly.

The boys were soaking up Wiley's faith commitments and examples.

After lunch the three went back to the Lasting Moments Floral Shop to pick up the wedding flowers. Then they headed back for the hospital.

To their delight, Annabelle was awake and talking to Angela when they walked in. It was very hard for the boys to air-hug their mom so they didn't hurt her. They were so elated that the drugs had somewhat worn off, and they could talk to their mother. Both were crying with relief as they told her about the shopping they had just done with Wiley.

They showed her the bridal bouquet, Angela's corsage and the boutonnieres – and told her how they would last forever – just like their new family. The boys showed Annabelle their new wedding suits and ties. She was really excited too as she told them everything was perfect.

"And now, Mom," Wilson blurted out, "Wiley has something to give you."

Wiley was grinning ear-to-ear as Wayne took the chain off of his neck and removed the engagement ring. Then put the chain back on his neck with the wedding band still hanging on it. He handed the ring to Wiley and nodded at his mom.

Jake, Angela and the boys watched intently as Wiley took the ring and knelt down beside Annabelle. As their eyes met, with a broken voice he asked her, "Annabelle, will you accept this ring as a token of my love for you as you become my wife?"

Annabelle rolled slightly up on her side as she smiled, "Yes Wiley, I 'cept yur ring an' will becom' yur wife."

With that Wiley slipped the ring on the ring finger of her left hand and kissed her gently. She looked at the ring, kissed it; then puckered her lips for another kiss from her fiancé.

"It's beautiful, Wiley, but it looks 'spensive. Yu didn' 'ave ta get me a fancy ring like this." She told him among kisses.

"I want you to have the best, you deserve it; and I'm sure glad your lips work without lipstick." Wiley chuckled at her.

Annabelle knew he was referring to the incident where she had painted lips all over her face. They were building memories.

"They cost seventy-five hundred dollars," Wilson blurted out, "but you did get a blue box with them. And, you can wear the rings on your left ring finger 'cause you'll be his wife. We'll have to wear ours on our right fingers 'cause only our wife's rings can be on our left ones." He held his fingers up to add emphasis to his description.

The boys both told her – at the same time –about the matching rings for the guys, and how their names will be engraved in them, even Wiley's, and that they will have diamonds too.

Jake and Angela were hugging each other, Wiley and the boys. What a beautiful afternoon. All is getting well.

Angela stepped over to Annabelle's bed as she asked her, "Is it all right if Jake an' I go an' pick you out a pretty weddin' dress?"

"I don' know if I cain get a dress on." Annabelle responded.

"I have an idea." Angela ensured as she whispered into her friend's ear.

Annabelle smiled as she nodded in agreement.

As they approached their big bike, Angela was clutching her husband's arm as she spoke, "I wanna go ta The Bridal Boutique an' see Zoe. She'll be able to do what I wan' done."

Jake nodded in agreement, then after a few delicious kisses they put their helmets on and took off.

Zoe recognized her as they walked in and asked her how her wedding was. Angela told her it was really exciting, and how she had an almost double wedding with her second bestus friend – now that her husband is her first bestus friend.

As she explained the weddings Zoe was looking comically at Angela, and Zoe caught the twinkle in Jake's eyes. He was smiling at his wife's description of the festivities too

Zoe started smiling too as she asked Angela, "What can I do for you today, Mrs. Judd?"

"We have Jake's secon' bestus friend's soon to be wife in the hospital. He's my husband's secon' bestus friend 'cause I'm his first bestus friend now. I hav' an idea for a weddin' dress for her. Her name is Annabelle and she is a widow. I want powder blue silk since she cain't wear white 'cause she's been married before. I wan' it made into a caftan with big drag-thru-the-gravy sleeves that 'ill fit over 'er arms – an' Velcro in the back like you did for my mom's dress."

Angela's hands and arms were making all sorts of moves as she was explaining what she had in mind, "She has ta get it over 'er bandaged head, arms an' back. But if the Velcro goes all the way ta the top, it won' 'ave ta go over 'er head, otherwise it'd be hard. I wan' some tiny white roses 'roun' the neck. The dress needs ta be big, but short, cause she only comes up to here on me." Angela informed Zoe as she pointed to her eyebrow, "I'm five-foot-six, so Annabelle's only 'bout five-foot-three. I wan' slippers ta match the dress, an' a turban with a veil put on it."

"Let's look at the swatches I have on silk I have in stock. Here's a nice power blue with small gold threads in it to make it shimmer," Zoe told Angela as she held up the swatch, "as for the turbans, all we have are these satin ones."

Angela looked at her supply and decided a slightly darker blue one would be okay.

"Can ya match the color of the veilin' to the dress?" Angela asked Zoe.

"Yes, I have the matching netting, how long do you want it?" Zoe responded.

Angela moved her hand up and down her bodice as she was seeing how it would work in her mind's eye.

Finally, she told Zoe, "Jus' below the shoulders will be fine. Don' wan' her to get tangled up in it. I wan' tiny white roses on the turban too please."

"I can sure do that." Zoe assured Angela.

Angela saw some pretty blue satin slippers, with the same gold threading as was in the dress material, so she told Zoe, "These'll be perfec', an' we'll need that special soft stuff in 'em to make 'em comfortable like mine were, an' some tiny white roses on them. We'll pick 'em up tomorrow."

"I – I'm not sure I can have them ready by tomorrow, Angela, Zoe said apologetically, "I don't know who can make the dress and headpiece that fast."

"What will it cost to find someone to make them by tomorrow afternoon? I'll pay whatever is necessary." Jake cut in.

"Well, I do have one seamstress who works out of her home – by the hour – but she charges thirty dollars an hour, and we're looking at about seven or eight hours of work." Zoe responded.

"So be it. It that's what my wife wants, that's what my wife gets. Tell your seamstress there's a fifty -dollar bonus, just get it done." Jake insisted.

Zoe excused herself and went to the back. She came out a few minutes later and told them they would be able to pick up the wedding gear tomorrow afternoon about three o'clock.

Legal Work

Annabelle was trying again to move up on her side so she could better talk to everyone, but Wiley could see her wince and pleaded with her to not move too much. It seemed like she couldn't take her eyes off her engagement ring. Wiley knew the boys and he had picked winners in the rings.

Wayne picked Annabelle's cell out of it charging cradle and headed for the Critical Care waiting room. Wilson was right on his tail. Wayne pulled up the Contact List and scrolled down to Pastor John Stoddard's number, the pushed the green button.

On the second ring Pastor John answered.

"Hello Pastor, this is Wayne, will you come day after tomorrow and marry us?"

There was a pause before Pastor John replied, "Where should I come, Wayne, and what time?"

"About four o'clock at the hospital here in the City. We got everything but the *Marriage License,* and I'm going to take care of that first thing in the morning." Wayne answered with authority.

"And how do you propose to get a Marriage License, you mom has to sign for it." Pastor John inquired of him.

"I know, but Jake gave me an idea, so I'll take care of it." He assured the pastor.

Two minutes later Jake's cell rang. It was John Stoddard asking Jake if he was aware of what was happening. Jake assured John he was aware of what is going on, but not how Wayne intends to get around the Marriage License dilemma. But they will just sit tight. Since Wayne told John that he was going to take care of it in the morning, Jake would call John tomorrow afternoon and fill him in.

"I think that kid is like Wiley already." Jake was saying.

"Yea," John answered, "really putting faith into action."

Wayne went back into Annabelle's room and asked Angela if he could talk to her.

She readily agreed. The two boys, flanked by Angela, went back to the waiting room, where Wayne asked for Jess's telephone number. Angela punched it in on her cell and handed it to Wayne; then she put Jess's number in Annabelle's cell.

As Jess answered Wayne told him what had been going on, and he needed to know what to put into their vows. Wiley had told him they couldn't be actual marriage vows because that's only for a husband and wife. So, he wanted Jess to make some vows for them to marry Wiley. Jess took down Annabelle's cell number and told Wayne he would call him back after while.

About an hour later Wayne's cell rang, and it was Jess. Both boys took off for the waiting room. Jess had come up with *Bonding Vows*, and he read them to Wayne. Then Wilson wanted to hear them too, so Jess read them to Wilson also. Both boys loved the vows, and asked Jess to give them to Pastor John to bring with him.

Jess inquired what they were going to do about Annabelle's signature on the *Marriage License.* Wayne told him Jake had given him an idea, and he was going to do the idea with faith – 'cause faith had brought his mom back. Wayne briefly told Jess what he was up to, and Jess thought it might work – especially with prayer and faith.

Angela was telling Annabelle about the dress, turban and slippers as the boys walked back in. Annabelle could tell by the sheepish grins that her boys were up to something, and that they had the look of having things under control. She asked them what they were up to, and they said it was a surprise. Wiley was grinning at his two Ronson boys, doing what needed to be done. He knew they were working on more wedding plans. He is so impressed at how industrious they are. I guess that comes from having to live by the skin of their teeth, and figure out ways to survive that seem impossible.

Jake and Angela took the two boys back to the motel with them; they would sleep in their own room with a regular bed tonight. Jake had rented the room next to them. The boys both felt very grown up – having their own motel room. A door made them adjoining rooms; Jake wanted that for safety. The boys wanted the door closed, but Jake said they had to leave it open at least an inch. It took several moments of communication between the two boys before they both agreed that the door was now ajar exactly one inch.

Jake could hear the shower running, and running, and running. Then the cradle of the telephone was picked and Wayne ordered some bedtime snacks. Jake looked at Angela and both started laughing. The boys were certainly making the most of having their own room.

About six o'clock in the morning Jake and Angela were sitting at the corner table in their room when the boys bounded in.

"We need to go to the Court House." Wayne informed Jake.

Jake looked at Wayne a couple of minutes before he answered; "OK, but first you boys need some breakfast, so let's go to the hospital cafeteria."

During breakfast they decided that Angela would wait in Annabelle's room while Jake and the boys went to the courthouse. They would take Wiley's Jeep, and Wiley would get some much-needed sleep.

When they walked into her room, their mom had her bed's head raised up a bit, and was almost all the way on her side. She smiled at them as she held out her bandaged arms to give her boys hugs. Gently they both lingered in the warm – ultra soft – hug from their mother. Wiley had sat up with Annabelle again all night, reading the Bible to her and praying.

"Back to the gurney with you Wiley Ronson," Jake told him, "my wife will be with Annabelle until we get back. I'll wake you then. I think you need to be in good shape for whatever the boys have planned for today. I need your Jeep keys."

Wiley gave both boys a hug, and walked to the gurney without coercion as he tossed his keys to his big faithful friend.

As the three walked into the courthouse, Wayne took the lead like he knew exactly where he was headed. They stepped into a small courtroom, and Wayne and Wilson headed for a door in the back, so Jake followed. As Wayne peeked his head in and started bowing, Jake heard a chuckle come from inside.

"Wayne, come on inside, is Wilson with you?" Jake could hear the jovial voice of Judge Barton say, "How's your mom?"

Both boys kept bowing as Wayne continued, "She's awake now Mr. Judge Sir, and Wiley got her the engagement ring and gave it to her."

"It cost seventy-five hundred dollars. And Wiley got us our wedding rings too; and there is a real diamond in them, and he's having our names put in them with our new name of Ronson. But we have to wear them on this finger 'cause only our wife can put them on this finger when we get big and married." Wilson blurted out as he held up his two ring fingers in question. "We've already picked out the flowers and Angela got a dress ordered, and a hat with a veil to cover her face."

"That's wonderful boys," Judge Barton responded, "now what can I do for you?"

"Well, Mr. Judge Sir," Wayne continued, "we need to get the license, but Mom can't get up yet to go sign for it. Jake said you being powerful might be able to help us."

"Yea," Wilson chimed in, "if an unconscious third-person with clouds can sign the power thing they can sign for my mom, and you're a cloudy unconscious person."

Both the judge and Jake started laughing.

"Hello Your Honor," I'm Jake Judd, "I will be the boy's Godfather as soon as they and Wiley are married."

"Hello Mr. Judd," Judge Roy Barton greeted Jake, "you must be related to young Jess Judd that was in my court room a few days ago. What is it the boys are looking for?"

"Yes Sir, Jess is my younger brother. I understand there is an *Affidavit of Identity* that along with a *Power of Attorney*, for the signing of the *Marriage Certificate* on her behalf, might be a way to get Wiley and Annabelle's *Marriage License.*

The judge thought a few moments, then called his secretary in as he said to her, "Miss Hall, please cancel the rest of my day, I've got some important business to take care of. Also, please bring me an *Affidavit of Identity* for and a *Limited Power of Attorney* form. I think this cloudy unconscious person just might be able to help."

Piper Hall told him she would be back in about five minutes.

"I'll have my car brought up from the basement so we can make a trip to the hospital." The judge told Jake.

"I've got Wiley's Jeep just outside, so if it's all right with you, Sir, we can take it." Jake replied.

"A Jeep?" The judge asked.

"Yes Sir, an open Jeep." Jake informed him.

"Well, it might be fun to ride in a Jeep again, been a long time since I've felt like a kid. Sounds like a plan." The judge agreed, gazing slightly into the wild blue yonder as if a pleasant thought was creeping into his head from a past experience.

It was less than five minutes when Miss Hall reappeared with the papers in her hand. The judge stuck them in his brief case, along with a stamp.

"I'm ready." Judge Barton announced, and the four headed for the Jeep.

The boys were skipping all the way.

Jake could tell the judge was really enjoying the ride, like a kid. He had a whimsical smile on his lips, and Jake could almost hear his thoughts going back to his days of youth. Like everyone in the world, Judge Barton has his own story.

When the four walked into Annabelle's room, Wiley was up again and sitting beside her bed. The big man stood up fostering a big smile.

"Wiley, this is Judge Roy Barton. Judge, this is Wiley

Ronson." Jake said as he made the introductions.

Wiley reached his right arm out to shake hands with the judge as he said, "Judge Barton, what a pleasure, my boys say you are the most wonderful judge in the world. I am honored!"

"With what your boys tell me, I am the one who is honored." Judge Barton responded shaking the big man's hand. "And this is Annabelle I assume?" As he carefully shook her hand.

"Sorry I can' stan' up fur ya, yur honor; but my mind is standin' up." She smiled at him.

"Your boys are really something, I adore them both." The judge told her.

"Than' ya so much Yur Honor, they's good boys." She was telling the judge as Wilson cut in and took his mom's hand to show the judge the ring.

"My, that's a mighty fine piece of jewelry Wilson." The judge agreed.

"We picked the rings out, Mr. Judge Sir, 'cause they got hearts on them and Mom has Wiley's heart." Wilson grinned.

Wilson showed the judge the flowers they had picked out, and their wedding clothes.

"I understand we have a bit of a legal hang up we need to fix?" Judge Barton remarked, "I think I can take care of everything – as long as I am invited to the wedding."

"My goodness, absolutely, Annabelle and I would be greatly honored to have such a distinguished gentleman join our celebration." Wiley informed him.

"My two grandkids are way back East, and I rarely get to see them; the only kids I seem to see are ones that have behavioral problems and I have to be a judge. These boys are so much fun to be around, it's such a treat. Wiley, you are one lucky man!"

"Yes Sir, I surely am." Wiley agreed.

The judge went on, "Will you allow me to be their God-Grandfather, like Jake will be their Godfather? Then when you come to the City we can go out and eat…and maybe play some video games…if they'll teach me."

"Wow, wow!" Was all the boys could say.

"Now, I need to get some information from you Annabelle. I have some questions. First, you want to marry Wiley of your own free will, and without duress. It is your conscious and willing decision?' The judge asked her almost snickering as he was remembering Wilson's calling him a cloudy unconscious person.

"Yes Sir, Your Honor, ain't nobody makin' me marry Wiley. I love him, an' so does my boys." Annabelle assured him.

"Good, now I need to know your full name; your mother and father's full names; your place of birth and birthdate. Also, I need to see your Citizenship papers if you were born in another country; and your late husbands Certified Death Certificate." The judge told her.

Wayne picked up the burned can with all the papers and opened it. He handed the papers to Judge Barton, who perused them carefully before he said. "Looks like everything's in order Annabelle. This first paper is a *Limited Power of Attorney*; it gives me the right to sign your name for the Marriage License only. You need to sign it right here, and Jake and his wife can witness your signature.

"This second paper is an application for a Standard Public Marriage License, you will sign it and I will witness your signature. Then Wiley and I will take it to the County Clerk's Office where we will finish filling out the forms, show all your proof of citizenship and right to marry. I will sign on your behalf with your Limited Power of Attorney. Then Wiley can drop me off at my office, and I will wait for your call for my invitation to the wedding as soon as the time is set. Do you have any questions Annabelle?"

"No, Yur Honor Sir, I unerstan' an' I got no questions." Annabelle replied.

"Wayne," Judge Barton spoke directly to him, "I'm writing down my cell number so you can call me direct, and may I have yours? Be sure and not give it to anyone else. I hope you will call me once in a while and let me know how you and Wilson are doing. If I am in court – just leave a message and I will call you back."

"I promise, I won't give it to anyone, except…what about my dad? I don't want secrets from him." Wayne asked and agreed at the same time.

"Of course, your dad's okay. I don't want you to keep secrets from your dad either." The judge agreed.

After Wiley and the Judge left for the Clerk's office, Jake told Wayne he probably should call Pastor John and tell him everything is go, and what time the wedding will be tomorrow.

"Four o'clock," Wayne responded, "that'll give everyone time to get here. Now I need some cupcakes with white frosting for the wedding, some candy kisses for treats, and cans of soda for drinks. Sonny can bring my dad's galvanized tub with him in the morning in the back of the truck. Ira can ask Todd and Kelli to bring a CD with them and sing a weddin' song."

Jake shook his head and chuckled with how Wayne had thought of each tiny detail; he had remembered everything from his and Angela's wedding. This fine young man was already a Ronson at heart, doing what needed to be done; and making things happen. Tomorrow the two boys will be his Godsons and he and Angela will be proud Godparents.

Wayne called Pastor John, and Angela called Josie to fill them in and tell them the wedding will be at four o'clock tomorrow. Angela asked Mam to call Jess and tell him too, that their plan had worked.

Mam called back about an hour later with guest information.

John Judd couldn't get off work. His boss, Shep Caldwell, was out of town, but Sonny, Ira and Jani would be coming in Sonny's black truck – with the tub. Todd and Kelli would be coming in their Toyota, with music, Deputy Homer and Billy with them.

Jake knew his baby sister would be safe with his bro Ira. Besides, Sonny is now a Mountain Man who protects the ladies. Jess will be coming and bringing Beth.

Jake had a count of about twenty guests coming, so he talked the hospital into letting them use one of the downstairs meeting rooms - already set up with chairs, a display table and a speaker's table.

Annabelle could lie on the gurney that Wiley had been napping on; to be wheeled down stairs. She said she wanted to stand up for the ceremony, so Jake figured with gentle but firm help she would be able to stand for a few minutes, and he and Wiley would be on each side of her.

She could roll on her stomach to drop her feet off the bed. The gurney would be right beside her bed, so all she had to do was turn around and lean over on the gurney. Then when they got down to the meeting room she could again roll her feet of the bed and carefully stand up – after everyone were in their places.

Jess was bringing his digital camera and Barstow would probably have his too. Jake also knew Emily would have her DVD camera.

Wiley would call Drew Rhein as soon as he got back to the hospital so he could be at the wedding and the insurance would take effect immediately. Drew had said that since he has court ordered custody of the boys that they were indeed covered. Now Wiley's whole family will be protected. His insurance rates will increase but the grateful groom and father will be happy to pay extra for his family.

When Wiley stepped back into the room waving the *Certificate,* everyone clapped. He showed the *Marriage License* to his soon to be wife and she started crying tears of joy. Pretty soon everyone in the room was crying tears of joy, including the nurse, Tammy, who had witnessed so much of the scenario. It's so good to laugh and to cry together. A sorrow shared is only half a sorrow, but a joy shared is twice a joy.

Wiley called Drew to have all papers ready to sign. Wayne called Judge Barton. Angela called Mam. Jake called Ira and told him to tell Todd and Kelli. Wiley called Sonny. Jake called Jess and Deputy Homer. Jess would take Jani down the hill to meet up with Ira and Sonny at the ranch where he would pick up Beth. Wayne called Sonny to bring the tub, and to stop and put some ice in it when they reached the City. Then Wayne called Todd to bring the music and to give he and Kelli a personal invitation.

The telephone lines were burning up.

Jake and Angela left to pick up the flowers, and stop by the jewelers to pick up the three men's rings. They would stop at the market and order cupcakes, pick up water, sodas and candy kisses. They would also pick up napkins, small plates, plastic forks and a book of matches.

Then they stopped by the Wedding Boutique to pick up the dress, headpiece and slippers, and get a unity candle and two side candles. Pastor John would be bringing the Communion Condiments.

Jake took the boys down to the cafeteria while Wiley and Angela helped Annabelle roll out of bed for the first time. She winced several times, but finally had her feet touching the floor. She kept a hold of Wiley's belt for stability as she stood up facing him.

"I feel yur heart poundin' Wiley." She said to him softly.

He was so emotional he couldn't speak as he stared down at her. She was standing up, and she was, with God's help, making all his dreams come true.

"Well, ya big lug, ar' ya gonna kiss me or not?" She teased.

Oh yes, he was gonna, and he did.

The dry run had gone very well. They would get her up again later that evening, and a couple of times in the morning to be sure she would be up to her wedding walk. Annabelle was upright.

Annabelle told Nurse Tammy Lane that she wanted to walk later in the evening, and Wiley would be there with her so she wouldn't fall. Tammy agreed she would be willing to try it if Mr. Ronson was right there.

"Where in the world did you find Mr. Ronson?" Tammy asked Annabelle.

"In church." Annabelle answered.

"Do you go to church, Tammy? Wiley asked her outright.

"No, I did when I was really little, but I just sort of got away from it when I got so busy." Tammy replied, "Besides, I don't think God likes people like me."

"You know, Tammy, God is never too busy for you. He loves

you, and you can talk to Him anywhere, about anything and at any time. You are still His little girl, no matter what you have haunting you." Wiley told her gently.

"When Annabelle first came in, none of us thought she would live, but then we watched as you and your boys literally prayed her back to life. We're all amazed." Tammy told Wiley.

"God is amazing, Tammy, and we sure would like to have you join us for our wedding tomorrow. I know you will be blessed." Wiley invited her.

That night when the family did their Bible study and prayer, they would be thanking their Lord for all of the blessings He had bestowed upon them – and pray for Tammy's Salvation and return to Christ.

Back in *Raincroft* two finely dressed men showed up at the *Rainrest Motel*, they signed in for one week. Finely tailored suits said they were men of influence. They signed in the license plate with a Federal ID number. They wouldn't give telephone numbers, said they were incommunicado, and the numbers were very private. They paid in cash.

Donna thought the license looked strange as she verified the plate on the vehicle and wrote down the car's description.

The young lady was somewhat frightened of their official looks, and as they quickly flashed gold badges at her, they kept staring at her.

They had signed in as George Jones and Ray Smith. George was almost bald, and Ray had lots of wavy dark hair. They were both about six-feet tall and Donna guessed they must each weigh about two-hundred pounds. She tried to make a mental note of their looks as she was wishing Sonny was there.

When they took their very dark glasses off she could see they both had brown eyes that seemed to pierce right into her as they kept staring at her hat and veil.

The stares made her very uncomfortable, and she was afraid to ask them to let her have a closer look at the badges to see what they really said.

There was a tattoo on George Smith's right wrist as his shirt pulled up a bit when his arm bent to sign her form. It said ***"Lamia"***. She didn't know the word, but wrote it down on the back of the sign-in form so she wouldn't forget it as soon as they left the counter. She also made notes of their looks and dress on the back of the forms. She wrote that she felt something was fishy, and was very uneasy, even though they said they were Federal agents taking a break.

She gave them each a key to room fifteen. It had two queen beds in it along with a table and two wing chairs by the front window facing the street – they had requested a front room, so they could keep an eye on their vehicle.

When the two men brought in some suitcases from their vehicle, the bags looked very heavy; especially two that were about four feet long.

A small figure was moving through the shadows, from behind one tree to another. The darkness of the night was hiding the little figure that walked up to the postal mail boxes and inserted a key into Box 28. As the door swung sideways an envelope was staring out at her. She picked up the envelope and stuck it in her pocket, re-locked the door and quickly headed back for the shadows.

Sonny had gotten home and was sitting at the desk going over her notes when she returned. He asked her why she had left the motel unattended. She ignored his question. Then he asked her about the men in fifteen and she told him how creepy they made her feel.

They also briefly talked about four other rooms that had been rented for the night.

Even though it was late, Sonny decided he would call Sheriff Leo and let him know about the two ambiguous strangers, their vehicle numbers and description – and the tattoo. The sheriff assured Sonny that it was never too late to call him with situation such as his, and thanked him for the information.

The sheriff told Sonny he would get back to him with any information he found. Sonny also told the sheriff he wouldn't be reporting to his office in the morning; that he wanted to see the strangers himself as they left – if they do – and perhaps figure out what they were up to. He was also heading to the wedding in the City. He asked Leo if he would keep an eye on his sister and the motel.

Leo said he'd be glad to watch things, and for Sonny to be very careful.

Not being sleepy, Sonny decided to work a bit on the big printing machine. He now had the motor running on it and found an old American Standard name on it. He had written to several companies that he had pulled up on the computer, and hoped one of them would know about the machine, and where he would be able to order some instructions and inking supplies for it. Sonny had made a decision about what to do with it.

The roof and exterior walls on Buildings one and Two of the *Canyon Casas* were finished. He and his two workers, Ronnie Baker and Max Monroe, had been working on them every day. Todd Carson was spending quite a bit of time working also.

Both Todd and Sonny had personal reasons for wanting to finish the project fast. His fellow cellmates were learning a trade, and were really enjoying the feeling of accomplishing something constructive. They both seemed to relish doing men's work in lieu of grunt work for other townspeople.

The views of the forest and Judd Canyon were awesome and peaceful. The four men would take breaks and sit on the top ledge of the canyon talking. Todd would go to the dollar menu and bring back sandwiches and sodas. Ronnie and Max seemed to almost forget they were on jail duty.

Jake had told Sonny he would be rewarding the two helpers, but hadn't said what he was going to do for them.

Of course, they had questions for Todd about his surprise marriage, and how he liked being a married man. Todd Carson was one happy man. Knowing where his final destiny would be at his death, having a gorgeous wife and soon to have a new home. He told them how he had never imagined how finding The Lord would give him such peace.

The guys listened intently when this rugged Mountain Man would talk about being peaceful. And his phrase "morality is macho" was sticking in their minds. Todd Carson was a real 'macho man' – and they didn't take his phrase lightly. He would remind them to consider what he's been blessed with for remaining macho.

Sonny felt his past actions with the ladies, could never be cleaned up. He knows Jake told him he could be a "God Virgin," and he's totally committed to that – but being the idiot he was with his conquests – he really didn't think that could apply to him.

Sonny was still learning everything about everything and anything he could take in off his computer. He had decided he really likes doing construction work. He had talked to Josie again about helping him get his General Equivalence Diploma (GED) so he could take some college classes. She was already schooling Todd, Ira and Deputy Homer, and Sonny would start with her next week using his computer at the Rainrest.

Studies right now for the trio right now included how to speak correctly – in English, pronouncing T's and D's without whining. Their penmanship was also being practiced. Ira was concentrating on how to make correct and legible numbers, and was also working in the afternoons and evenings with Lenore, and loving it.

Josie was impressed at how quickly Homer learns everything.

"The Deputy is really smart." Josie told her husband – and Jani. "Homer doesn't miss a thing, and has a fantastic memory. He hears something one time and he's got it."

Josie had received her *State Education Teaching* Certificate when she was home schooling her own children, and has kept up with all the required schooling to keep her *Certification* current and in-tact.

When Donna got to her room, she pulled her hat off and gazed at the return address printed on the envelope. It said '*Airman Michael Crabtree.*' As she opened it, there was an air of excitement in her. She couldn't remember ever getting anything addressed to her before. It felt strange for her to see her own name on a piece of paper - that someone else had written.

She pulled the paper out of the envelope and started reading, it said: "Greetings Donna. I arrived here to the Air Force Base safely. That was the first time I had ever been in an airplane, and it was sort of scary. Have you ever been in an airplane? The cars below looked like little ants, and the roads like a crossword puzzle. I did enjoy the scenery though.

"The attendant pulled down what I later found out was an oxygen mask and started telling us how to use it. At first, for one frightening moment – I was freaked out. I thought the plane was in crisis. It was sure a relief when I found out it was only a demonstration.

"I guess I will have eight and one-half weeks of Basic Training, then I will go somewhere for technical training of some kind. I've been thinking about computer repair. We don't, to my knowledge, have a computer repairman there in *Raincroft*.

"I hope my sister Angela and her new husband, Jake, are enjoying their honeymoon. I miss everyone; living with all strangers will take a bit of getting used to.

"After basics I will be able to get my own place while I'm in school.

"Your friend, Mike"

She re-read the letter several times. It said, "Your friend", she had never had a friend before. Maybe sometime she would tell him she signed the Guest Registers at both weddings that day, and he was standing there right by the Guest Book on the second wedding talking to someone and didn't even see her slip in.

There was an old man standing with the Guest Book on the first wedding, and he just looked at her funny. She had just signed 'Donna', but it still made her feel a part of something.

The beauty of Angela Crabtree, Mike's big sister, had mesmerized her. In fact, she had been almost frozen at the door of the sanctuary and had stood there so long that she was sure several people had seen her.

Donna put her black hat and veil back on and slipped quietly out of her bedroom window and into the darkness.

Nurse Tammy stopped in Annabelle's room and asked her if she was ready to get up and walk now. As Tammy looked over at Wiley, he smiled and nodded. Annabelle was halfway slid off the bed by the time the two attendees got to her. When her feet touched the floor, she grabbed Wiley's belt for stability. He took hold of her sides just underneath her arms, and walked backward as she took a couple of steps. Then she took a few more steps.

"I feel good," she told her smiling fiancée, "I wanna walk some more."

She reached for Wiley's hands and he slowly backed up toward the door, and his wounded little lady followed him. She too was smiling; she was walking on her own, and it felt wonderful.

Annabelle wanted to practice once more before bedtime, and again twice in the morning so she could walk up the aisle to her new husband at her wedding tomorrow. Her two sons could walk her down the aisle, one on each side, to stabilize her, and give her hand to Wiley.

Jake said he would follow them down the aisle – just in case.

A Wedding, A Bonding & Godparents

Today was their wedding day, and the bride and groom were awake early. Most of the pain medications had worn off, and Annabelle wasn't dizzy like she had been. The pain was still pretty intense.

The day nurse walked in to help her out of bed for her first walk of the morning. The wounded lady was ready as she reached for Wiley's hand for stability.

"At this rate I can go home now." Annabelle told the nurse, who didn't respond.

Step by step, Annabelle was getting her equilibrium, and now she just wanted one of Wiley's arms. She wanted to walk beside him instead of facing him as he backed around. He held his arm out to her, and she took it as they slowly started for the door. They were going to walk a short way down the hall.

Wiley could feel her getting tired, and even though she wouldn't admit to it, he headed her back toward her bed. The nurse would now clean her wounds and put fresh bandages on them, and on Wiley's. The walk was another success.

The big man mentioned to the nurse about trying a wheel chair with a thick spongy pad in both the seat and against the back. As Wiley mentioned that to the nurse, Annabelle honed in on the statement and asked the nurse to please bring a chair in about an hour. She was determined to get out of that bed.

Jake, Angela and the boys showed up. Annabelle was telling

them how she walking in the hall, and in a bit she would be trying out a wheel chair.

Angela was carrying the pretty blue sack lettered Bridal Boutique. Jake nodded to Wiley to go with him out of the room. He couldn't see the dress before the wedding.

Reluctantly Wiley agreed, and the two men went down to the cafeteria. The boys wanted to stay with Angela and see their mom's reaction to her wedding dress.

Angela took the gold box out of the blue sack, and pulled the lid off of it. Annabelle's eyes got as big as dollars; she loved the color, and the golden threads woven through the fabric. Angela held the dress up to Annabelle as she rubbed her fingers extending beyond the bandages over the beautiful material to feel how soft and silky it was. Then Angela held up the slippers to match, and the turban with the veil. Annabelle's heart was so full of happiness and gratitude that she couldn't even speak.

'She likes 'em," Wilson announced, "I can tell."

Yes, Annabelle loved her wedding clothes; she would be a real bride, with flowers and a veil and all the trimmings. And this time she would be marrying for love.

She had a sheepish grin on her lips when Wiley walked back in, and she reached for his hand to kiss it; then pulled him down so she could taste his lips.

The nurse came back with the wheel chair that sported six-inch soft foam pads on the seat and back, covered by a soft sheet blanket. Wiley was antsy as he helped his soon to be wife stand up and turn around to back down in the chair. He could see her wince and wanted her to stop and just walk instead. But Annabelle was determined, and slowly and carefully started to sit down. She bolted forward just a bit and Wiley's heart sank. Ignoring the pain, she settled back down bit by bit until she had her bottom on the cushion. She didn't lean back, that would have to come later, but she was sitting up.

"Now I cain go forwar' ta my weddin', an' ride home" She told Wiley, who was so proud of her courage and determination.

Annabelle wanted Wiley to push her around the halls, so he did, and her entourage followed.

Sonny, Ira and Jani showed up about two o'clock, they didn't want to be late.

The boys wanted to show Jani the cafeteria after she took Wiley's wedding clothes up to Annabelle's room.

Sonny was filling Wiley and Jake in on the Casas situation, and the Ronsons new home. He and his helpers had even erected the stem walls under the building. It was ready for occupancy.

The big men thanked him for all his help, and told him how much they appreciate him. Sonny asked Wiley where the meeting room was so he could put the ice filled tub in out of the sun. Sonny would back the truck up to the door and he and Ira would carry it into the meeting room.

Nurse Tammy had come into the room and said she would be glad to show Sonny and Ira where the room is.

Angela had secretly picked up some extra ribbon, two white plastic lace looking tablecloths, tie bands and big blue roses from Zoe. Jake was filling the tub with the soda when the two ladies walked back into the room. Angela sat the sack from the Bridal Boutique on the speaker's table, and emptied it out. She and Jani started making bows out of the ribbon. Angela hadn't thought about scissors, but a nurse watching the proceedings handed hers to Angela.

The girls decorated the inside aisle ends of the rows of chairs with the big white bows adorned with blue roses. They set up the speaker's table with one of the plastic lace tablecloths for the Communion and Unity Candle table. The second tablecloth was put on the display table by the wall for the cupcakes and candy kisses, along with the napkins, forks and small plates. Sonny said he would go pick up the cupcakes.

Jake pulled the side table out from the wall so the couple could be standing behind it facing the guests. That would also let Annabelle's wheelchair get behind the table for the cake eating part of the ceremony. The room was lovely.

The boys were wondering where Angela and Jani had disappeared to, and went looking for them. When they walked into the meeting room they were overjoyed. It was a really wedding looking room. Wayne thanked the ladies for their help. Wilson would have, but he as too busy looking at how the blue roses were fastened to the ribbon and the chairs. Angela also made bows for each end of the 'treats' table.

And now the waiting. Since the boys had gotten dressed in their fancy duds at the crack of dawn, Jake told them to wait at the entrance door of the hospital and direct people into the wedding room, and be sure everyone had their correct flowers on. Jake knew they didn't need to be there while the ladies got Annabelle in her wedding dress.

He also knew he'd have to pry Wiley out of the room as soon as he had his suit on. He knew his wife; little sister and Nurse Tammy could handle what was to be done in Annabelle's room.

Todd, Kelli, Billy and Deputy Homer arrived about two-thirty. After getting properly 'flowered' by the boys, Todd went to set up the CD player and Kelli went up to Annabelle's room. Todd had brought a non-verbal CD of love songs with him to play in the background as people arrived. He and Kelli would be singing. "From This Moment on" by Shania Twain for their love song.

By three o'clock Pastor John, Emily, Elder Barstow and Mia were there. Pastor John wanted to talk to Wiley and his family before the ceremony, so John called the boys from the front door to go upstairs with him and Emily. Pastor John also wanted to talk to Jake and Angela to be sure everyone was on the same page.

Wiley was just finishing dressing in the bathroom and came out when he heard Pastor's voice. The two men hugged, as did Emily and Annabelle.

Mia and Barstow stayed downstairs to help put the cupcakes and treats out on the table. Barstow also wanted some pre-wedding photos of everything. The Judd's had ordered four dozen cupcakes. They thought there might be a few extra people slip into watch the proceedings.

Pastor John handed Wiley the Wedding Vows he had prepared for the actual Marriage Ceremony, then the Bonding Vows the boys had put together with Jess. He handed Jake and Angela a copy of a Godfather Certificate Jess had made up for them as they accepted the responsibility of becoming the boys' Godparents.

"I will be doing Wiley and Annabelle's Marriage Ceremony

first, then the *Bonding Vows,* followed by the *Godparent Confirmation Vows.* The *Bonding* and *Confirmation Vows* are not Legal documents; but spiritual and moral ones." The Pastor informed everyone.

Wiley softly read the *Bonding Vows* for the boys to Annabelle and then the *Marriage Vows.* "Are these all ok with you, Baby? Do you want anything reworded or changed?" He asked her.

"No Wiley, they ar' 'xactly perfect. Ya sure look han'some. Jus' thin', another hour an' we'll be married." Annabelle said joyfully as the bride and groom took a couple of moments to smooch.

"Okay, Wiley," Jake intersected, "dressing time, so all men need to go to the meeting room." Wiley stood there a moment longer, but Jake took his arm to walk out with him.

"Next time you see her Wiley," Jake continued, "it will be as your bride coming to you. Don't worry, my friend, the ladies can handle getting her ready for you."

Jake sent the boys' back to the front doors to greet guests, and finish their 'flower duty.' Kelli went back down to be with her husband.

As Judge Roy Barton got to the doors of the hospital, both boys opened them for him and started bowing. The judge gave each boy a hug as they tried to both pin the flower on his lapel at the same time. They took his hands and walked him right up to the front row to sit. Wiley and Jake walked over to the Judge and introduced Pastor John Stoddard to him.

Pastor John showed the judge the papers that had put together for the *Bonding* and *Godparent* ceremonies and told him he knew they weren't legally binding, but spiritually and morally, and will be a witness to all present exactly what Wiley and Annabelle's wishes are in the event of their demise.

The judge was impressed as he inquired; "Did young Jess Judd have anything to do with these?"

"He sure did." Pastor John affirmed.

"My, Jess is an intelligent young man. I'd like to get to know him better." The judge added.

Emily had been videoing everything going on in the meeting room and as much as was decent in the bride's room. Barstow's camera was clicking non-stop. The newlyweds would have many memories to look back on.

Nurse Tammy helped Annabelle stand up, and as soon as she was comfortable that her patient was solid, she let go of her. She stayed steady, so Angela and Jani took her dress out of the box, took off her hospital gown, and slid her wedding dress on her arms. They fastened the Velcro that made the back seam.

Next – her turban. It fit perfectly over her head and bandages, and the veil softly fell over her face and shoulders. "An' now little bride," Angela said to her, "we need ta get ya down in the chair so we can get yur slippers on."

It took a few moments, but after Annabelle finally was seated, Angela put her little blue slippers on. Annabelle was already in tears; she was still having a hard time believing that she would soon be marrying a man she really loves; not one someone else arranged for her to marry. And this wonderful man was adopting her two sons too.

The bride looked lovely. Angela wheeled her over to the long mirror on the bathroom door so she could see herself.

"Ooops, wait a minute," Jani declared, "the bride needs her bouquet."

Jani handed Annabelle her beautiful flowers. Now the bride was ready to go to her groom. Jani pinned Angela's corsage on her, and Angela pinned Jani's carnation on her. This was the first time the two sisters-in-law had seen each other since the wedding, and they were building a really great bond between them. They seemed to be able to read each other's thoughts already.

Emily was still running back and forth from the wedding room to the bride getting as much film as possible of every event. (Good thing Emily's in good health.)

At three-forty-five, the boys showed up in the doorway. Wayne wolf-whistled at his mom, and Wilson tried to – but all he could do was sputter.

"Mom, you're beautiful! Really beautiful!" Wayne told her.

"Looks like Wiley won't be getting his ugly wife now, Mom,"

Wilson cracked, "you don't even have to have a veil to cover your face."

The boys wanted to push their mom down to her wedding, so again her entourage followed as they started for the elevator. Other patients, and their guests, and medical staff were peeking out their doors and lining the hallway as they passed, clapping and giving their best wishes. Annabelle felt like a queen as she waved at everyone.

Soft romantic music could be heard as they approached the door of the wedding room. It was for her - Annabelle. Her heart felt like it was going to pop right out of her chest. She was so happy she didn't even notice the pain she experienced every time she moved.

To thin' o' where I comes from, an' how far Jesus has brot me is 'mazing. From a mud floor hutch, ta bein' a queen. Thoughts of great thanksgiving were running through her mind.

The boys stopped outside the door, and Nurse Tammy helped the bride to stand up and get stable. One boy stood on each side, and Jake came out in the hall to walk behind the bride.

When the door opened and Jani stepped into the aisle to walk in and sit down, Deputy Homer stood up. He soon realized she wasn't the Bride or Maid-of-Honor and sat back down – totally embarrassed. Everyone was giggling, and Jani grinned at him. Homer grinned back at Jani as Jake watched the sparks between them.

Then Angela started down the aisle to walk to the front and stand with the wedding party. Todd started the *"Wedding March"* as Annabelle stepped into the doorway, flanked by her two sons. Everyone stood up to watch as the bride passed by. Wiley was so excited that he started laughing right out loud as he clapped his hands. His deep boisterous laugh was contagious because everyone else started laughing and clapping too. This wounded little lady looked beautiful, and she was walking to her wonderful man.

When they reached the front Pastor John said, "Who gives this woman to be married to this man?"

Both boys answered together, "We – her sons – do."

And with that they placed their mother's right hand in Wiley's big strong hand. There didn't seem to be anyone else in the room as the bride and groom stared at each other.

Finally, Pastor John cleared his throat slightly to get their attention.

Jake stepped over to his wife, and they took each other's hands as remembrance flooded their minds.

"Dearly Beloved," Pastor John started, "we are gathered here to join this man and this woman in Holy Matrimony. If there is anyone who has ought against this marriage let them speak now, or forever hold their tongue."

The room was silent so Pastor John continued, "Let us pray. Almighty Father, maker of Heaven and Earth, we ask You to bless this union with health, love and commitment. Amen.

"I'll not do a sermonette today because of the bride's fragile condition. But let me say that it is Almighty God who ordained marriage. He has told us it is not good for man to be alone, and so He made man a helpmeet. A woman, someone very different; and yet very like man. Someone to laugh and cry with; to love and cherish.

"Wiley Ronson, in the presence of God and these friends, do you take this woman, Annabelle Close, to be your lawfully wedded wife, to live together in the Holy State of marriage, and promise with Divine assistance to be a loving and faithful husband, and next to The Lord keeping her first in your life for as long as you shall live?"

"I do." Wiley responded, smiling at his lady.

"Annabelle Close," Pastor John continued, "in the presence of God and these friends, do you take this man, Wiley Ronson, to be your lawfully wedded husband, to live together in the Holy State of marriage, and promise with Divine assistance to be a loving and faithful wife, and next to The Lord keeping him first in your life for as long as you shall live?"

"I do." Annabelle agreed, smiling back at the man becoming her husband at that very moment.

"The rings please." Pastor John said as he held his hand out.

The boys had each been holding one ring and they handed

them to the pastor at the same time as the pastor said, "As you can see the rings are round, they have no ending. That is how your relationship will be now; it will have no end in God's eyes.

"Wiley, please take this ring and place it on Annabelle's third finger of her left hand and repeat after me – with this ring I thee wed."

"With this ring I thee wed." Wiley said to Annabelle.

Pastor continued, "I give you this ring as a symbol of my love and faithfulness."

"I give you this ring as a symbol of my love and faithfulness." Wiley repeated still staring at his lady.

"I commit my heart and soul to you, and ask you to wear this ring as a reminder of the vows we have spoken today, our wedding day." Pastor stated.

Wiley repeated, "I commit my heart and soul to you, and ask you to wear this ring as a reminder of the vows we have spoken today, our wedding day."

"Annabelle, please take this ring and place it on Wiley's third finger of his left hand and repeat after me, with this ring I thee wed." Pastor instructed Annabelle.

"With this rin' I thee wed." Annabelle told Wiley.

"I give you this ring as a symbol of my love and faithfulness." Pastor said.

"I give ya this rin' as a symbol o my luv an' faithfulness." Annabelle repeated slowly trying to pronounce all the words.

"I commit my heart and soul to you, and ask you to wear this ring as a reminder of the vows we have spoken today, our wedding day." Pastor John continued.

"I commit my heart an' soul ta ya, an' ask ya ta wear this rin' as a reminder o the vows we 'ave spoken today, ar weddin' day." Annabelle repeated slowly to Wiley.

"And now," Pastor John announced, "with your pledges to each other in front of this body of friends, and the exchanging of rings, by the authority of Almighty God and the State of California, I pronounce that you are husband and wife. What God has joined together let no one separate. You may kiss your wife, Wiley."

"I love you Mrs. Ronson." Wiley said to his new wife as he lifted her veil and laid it back over her turban and kissed her softly.

"I love ya too Mr. Ronson." Annabelle said to her new husband as she kissed him back.

As the new man and wife headed for the Unity Candles, Todd and Kelli began singing their love song by *Shania Twain*; it was perfect.

"I do swear that I'll always be there.
I'd give anything and everything and I will always care.
Through weakness and strength, happiness and sorrow,
For better or worse, I will love you with every beat of my heart."

Wiley and Annabelle took the outside candles Barstow had lit and jointly lit the center Unity Candle, then extinguished their individual candles.

Since Annabelle could not kneel, Pastor John administered the Communion Condiments while they were standing at the Unity Candle table.

"Mr. and Mrs. Ronson will take the Sacraments of Christ Jesus as the first act of their marriage. I like to do this holy act using the words of **First Corinthians 11:23-27.** It says, *The Lord Jesus took bread, and after He had given thanks, He broke it and said, "Take, eat, this is My Body, which is broken for you; do this in remembrance of Me."*

"You may now break the wafer and eat it symbolizing the death of Christ on the cross as His Body was broken for us." Pastor instructed them.

"After the like manner He also took the cup, and when He had supped, He said, *"This cup is the New Testament in My Blood: this do ye, as oft as ye drink it, in remembrance of Me. For as often as ye eat this bread and drink this cup you show the Lord's death until He comes again."*

"You may now drink the cup that symbolizes the Lord's death and resurrection; done to atone for our sins." Pastor told them, then he turned to the audience as he added to them, "I charge each one of you to support this couple by the commandments of God. Do you each accept this charge?"

The audience all agreed.

Pastor then turned back to the newlyweds as he said, "I now present to you Mr. and Mrs. Wiley Ronson."

Everyone stood up and started clapping as Wiley and his wife smiled at each one in the audience, and at each other.

Tammy brought the wheel chair to the front of the wedding room, and she and Wiley helped Annabelle sit down to rest and watch the next ceremony.

"Now," Pastor John continued, "will Wayne and Wilson please take Wiley's hands. Wayne, will you please read your Bonding Vows to Wiley?"

"I, Wayne Allen Close, before God and these witnesses, take you Wiley Emerson Ronson, to be my Spiritually-Bonded-Father. I promise to love, honor and obey you for as long as I live." The young man recited.

"Wiley, will you please say your pledge to Wayne?" Pastor John inquired.

"I, Wiley Emerson Ronson, before God and these witnesses take you Wayne Allen Close to be my Spiritually-Bonded-Son. I promise to love, honor, provide for and protect you for as long as I live. With this ring I thee invest you as my heir with all rights of endowment." Wiley responded to his new oldest son as he slipped the ring on his finger.

"I, Pastor John Stoddard, in the eyes of God and these witnesses, now declare you Wiley Emerson Ronson and Wayne Allen Close, *Spiritual Father and Son,* in the name of the Father, the Son and the Holy Ghost. You may now hug each other.

"Wilson, will you please read your *Bonding Vows* to Wiley." Pastor said to Wilson.

"I, Wilson Andrew Close, before God and these witnesses, take you Wiley Emerson Ronson, to be my Spiritually-Bonded-Father. I promise to love, honor and obey you for as long as I live." Wilson pledged to Wiley.

"Wiley, will you please say your pledge to Wilson?" Pastor continued.

"I, Wiley Emerson Ronson, before God and these witnesses, take you Wilson Andrew Close to be my Spiritually-Bonded-Son. I promise to love, honor, provide for and protect you for as long as I live. With this ring I thee invest you as my heir with all rights of endowment." Wiley pledged to his new youngest son as he slipped the ring on his finger.

"I, Pastor John Stoddard, in the eyes of God and these witnesses, now declare you Wiley Emerson Ronson and Wilson Andrew Close, *Spiritual Father and Son* in the name of the Father, the Son and the Holy Ghost. You may now hug each other.

"You each have witnessed these *Bonding Vows* events. You each now know it is the desire of these three men to belong to each other in the eyes of God and man. As witnesses to this solemn event, in the case of the untimely demise of Wiley and Annabelle Ronson, these boys are to be his *Legal Heirs* and have all rights to his property, both Real and Personal. Do each one of you promise to protect these young men and their estate?" Pastor asked the audience.

Everyone present said, "I do."

"Now for our final ceremony of today," Pastor continued, "Jake and Angela Judd will you please take Wayne and Wilson's hands as I read your confirmation and acceptance of being their Godparents?

"This *Certificate of Godparent Commitment* states that you Jake and Angela Judd will faithfully:

Pray for your Godchildren regularly.

Set an example of Christian living for them.

Help the boys to grow in the faith of God the Father, Son and Holy Ghost.

Give every encouragement to follow Christ Jesus and fight against evil.

Accept financial responsibility for the boys in the event it becomes necessary.

Be there for them from this day forward in the small and great things.

Protect them."

Both Jake and Angela answered at the same time, "I will."

"Then I confirm you both as Godparents to Wayne and Wilson Close in the name of the Father, the Son and the Holy Ghost, and into the Lord Jesus. You may now hug both of your Godsons." Pastor announced smiling from ear to ear.

"Now mom and dad get to feed each other some cake." Wilson spoke up, as the boys headed for the treat table.

As Jake turned around to face the audience he was sure he saw tears in Sonny's eyes. The young man was deeply touched with what he had witnessed.

Wiley wheeled his wife's chair around behind the table, and helped her stand up. Then they each picked up a cupcake, peeled the wrappers off of them, and held the cakes up to each other's mouths as Barstow was snapping pictures – along with everyone else – even the judge.

The newlyweds were giggling so hard they could hardly feed each other.

Wayne opened two Ginger Ale cans and set them in front of his parents for their toast. Then both boys passed out sodas to all the guests, including several that had just dropped in.

When everyone had a soda and cupcake, Jake picked up his can and held it up in the air to make the toast. "I want to personally congratulate Wiley and Annabelle Ronson for all they have come through, and for this special and wonderful day. I pray there will be many more happy days for the Ronson Family."

Everyone held up their sodas and shouted congratulations as the bride and groom gave each other a drink from the can – with great difficulty. Then the audience started tapping on their cans to tell the newlyweds to kiss each other again – and they gladly did.

Wiley's deep laugh could be heard occasionally above the softly playing music.

After all *Licenses and Certificates* were signed by everyone, including Drew's Insurance Papers, Wiley said his wife needed to get back to bed and get some rest, as he helped her sit down in the chair again. As soon as everyone had given their good wishes, and Wiley said a special thank you to the judge, Wiley took his wife toward the elevator asking his sons to be sure the meeting room was cleaned properly and all guests thanked.

As Nurse Tammy approached Angela to tell her she had never witnessed anything so moving before, Angela invited her to come to church; and told her Jake's old bedroom was available for her to spend the night in, or the *Rainrest Motel* was within walking distance to church. Tammy said she would consider coming sometime.

Several other medical personnel were lingering around the room too, like they didn't want to let the feelings they had felt get away.

Judge Barton stepped up to say his good-byes to the boys, Jess and Jake before he headed back to work, he was saying, "I've never witnessed a ceremony like that before, it was great. I think that family is going to be all right. I hope they keep in touch with this cloudy unconscious person, I feel like I have a personal stake in them now as the boy's God-grandfather. Since I met them I find myself seeing a more comical side of life, and I don't want to lose them. What they put together for this festivity is absolutely amazing."

"I'm sure they will keep in touch; the boys think you are the cat's meow." Jake assured him.

Then the judge gave each boy a big hug as he said his good-by, and telling them how blessed he was to witness their weddings. Then he stopped to talk a bit to Jess before he left asking Jess to let him know as soon as he passed the Bar Exam. Judge Barton also told the soon to be lawyer that he would be glad to give him a *Moral Character Reference* to be turned in with his final test application for the November *MPRE*. Jess agreed and thanked him profusely.

Jake and Angela stayed and helped the boys be sure the room was left clean. Then they would take the boys out to dinner, and maybe the Amusement Park, so the newlyweds could have some time alone.

Sonny took Jake aside and told him about the two strangers that had landed at the motel, and how he is very uncomfortable with them. He told Jake he had called the Sheriff and filled him in, and that Leo would be checking out the strange license plates on the black vehicle. Jake was glad for the information as he told Sonny, "Black is a good color for hiding in the dark…wonder what they are up to. Any idea what they might have in the heavy long suitcases?"

Sonny shook his head no, but they both knew very dangerous things could be hiding in them, and George's tattoo of "Lamia" added to the seriousness of the situation. Then Sonny told Jake about Deputy Homer standing up when Jani walked in. Jake told him he had witnessed it through the doorway, and both men laughed about it.

Deputy Homer asked Sonny if he would have Billy Carson ride back with him so Jani could ride back with Todd and Kelli. Sonny mentioned the deputy's request to Todd, who chuckled as he agreed, "We can probably work that out. You, Billy and Ira take off without any good byes – which will probably do the trick. Might be fun to watch the mesmerized deputy fumble for words while we're riding. Jani sure can't ride back with Jess and Beth."

Sonny smiled and nodded at Todd as he took off with the galvanized tub, and a nod to Ira and Billy. He was so glad that he and Todd and Ira were now friends.

The three men had come up missing as everyone else started leaving. Jani was telling her big brother that she had been left behind, that the guys probably figured she'd be riding back with Jake and Angela.

Jake caught Homer's slightly silly grin as he listened to his sister.

"You can ride with us, Jani." Todd told her with another silly grin Jake caught.

"Jani can't even be around Homer when Mam's schooling him; he goes all to pieces. He's an A+ student until she walks in." Jake informed Todd.

"I know." Todd snickered.

Deputy Homer was already waiting by Todd's Toyota.

As Wiley helped his wife stand up out of the chair, she didn't lie down on the bed; she wanted her husband to hold her close. She was able to raise her arms up enough to get them around his chest as she snuggled into him.

"I'm so happy." She purred to him.

"Me too, Baby, you've made all my dreams come true, and I love you with everything in me." He told her as he kissed her sweet lips that now belonged to him alone.

Annabelle just kept clinging to her husband. He was concerned about her being in pain, but she just wanted more and more kisses and closeness.

"Those are pretty sexy kisses." Wiley whispered in her ear as he accepted them.

"I know, but i's right an' proper now 'cause we's married." She reminded him.

It felt so good to be close to her husband, and she didn't want to go back to bed yet.

Seemed like forever since they had held each other.

Author's Bio

MYSTERY MOUNTAIN THREE is the third in the series of the sagas of the little town of *Raincroft* California. Mountain folk live deep within the heart of Marie. She loves the backward honesty of most of the wonderful people in *Raincroft*. The way the people look after each other would be a right and proper way for us to look after each other today.

We generally do not cause the horrendous things that befall us, like Annabelle being struck by lightning. That is when we must be strong, and look to our Creator and King, Jesus Christ, for the strength to endure what we must, however hard it may be.

The Author sincerely hopes you will grow in Jesus as you read all four of her books, *THOUGHTS APLENTY,* and her series *MYSTERY MOUNTAIN, MYSTERY MOUNTAIN TWO,* and this new one *MYSTERY MOUNTAIN THREE.*

MYSTERY MOUNTAIN FOUR is currently in the making, with lots of adventure; including a family in the Witness Protection Plan that the Cartel's find; and a young lady kidnapped and cuffed to a tree in the forest.

Look for it soon.

I Pray Blessings on each of you.

MARIE GRACE

MYSTERY MOUNTAIN THREE

MARIE GRACE

MYSTERY MOUNTAIN THREE

MARIE GRACE

MYSTERY MOUNTAIN THREE

www.ingramcontent.com/pod-product-compliance
Lightning Source LLC
Chambersburg PA
CBHW021143080526
44588CB00008B/201